C0-AVE-943

DREAMS TO REALITY

A Biography of
DR A.P.J. ABDUL KALAM

SRINIVAS LAXMAN

Illustrated by

PRABHAKAR WAIRKAR

NAVNEET PUBLICATIONS (INDIA) LIMITED

Price : Rs. 100.00

F 0551

© **Navneet Publications (India) Limited (2004)**

First Edition : February, 2004

All rights reserved. No part of this book may be copied, adapted, abridged or translated, stored in any retrieval system, computer system, photographic or other system or transmitted in any form or by any means without the prior written permission of the copyright holders. *Any breach will entail legal action and prosecution without further notice.*

Editors :

Coomi Chinoy
Subhra Mazumdar
Rizio Raj
Sathyanath Nair

Published by

Navneet Publications (India) Ltd.
Bhavani Shankar Road, Dadar,
Mumbai – 400 028, INDIA
Tel. (022) 6662 6565 ● Fax : (022) 6662 6470
e-mail : publications@navneet.com
Visit us at : www.navneet.com

ISBN 978-81-243-1274-2

Printed at : Paramount Litho & Offset Works, Mumbai 400 011.   1006

This Book is dedicated
to the apple of my eye —
my daughter **Rimanika**
who is my inspiration.
My mother **Kamala** and
my father **R. K. Laxman**,
who encouraged me and
my wife **Usha** who was the
driving force behind this project.

Dr A. P. J. ABDUL KALAM
PRESIDENT OF INDIA

FOREWORD

Many books have come out in recent years, up to now ten, on the life of Dr A.P.J. Abdul Kalam, President of India. The book most widely known is *Wings of Fire*, his autobiography which became a best seller. There are several other books : *India 2020*; and *Ignited Minds* written by him. However, all of these are for adults.

This book is for children. His interaction with the young has always given Dr Kalam great delight. He never misses an opportunity for this. Of all the Presidents of India, he is the one who can aptly be referred to as the 'Children's President'. It is very appropriate to have a book on his life that children will enjoy; and I am sure he will enjoy it too.

The book is written in an easy style for children to follow. Particularly attractive are the large number of illustrations which would endear it to children. Shri Prabhakar Wairkar needs to be congratulated for the quality of these which bring out so pithily the message of the text. I certainly prefer this to photographs for such a book.

When I was young I read two books each with a caption in the title : "Log Cabin to White House", there were additional words in the title to clarify who these books were about. The two books described how President Abraham Lincoln and President Garfield rose from small beginnings to become Presidents of the United States of America. In this respect our record in India is pretty good. Our Presidents have by and large come from humble beginnings to rise to the highest constitutional office in the country. President Kalam is no exception.

Dr Kalam rose to his present position through sheer hard work, dedication and a commitment to the objectives he had set himself. The book brings out how from success and failure he battled his way upward. This will have a significant influence on young minds, on how they can also succeed if they really try hard. On a larger scale that is also the message for the country.

I am privileged to write this Foreword for this first attempt at writing a book by Srinivas Laxman. The title *'Dreams To Reality'* is something that I have quoted in many talks; for the great Nobel Prize winning scientist Pierrie Curie, when asked what was his motto, had remarked "to make of life a dream and to turn the dream to reality".

(Prof. M.G.K. Menon, FRS)
Dr Vikram Sarabhai Distinguished Professor
Indian Space Research Organization

PREFACE

A few months after Dr Kalam became the President of India, a number of books about him hit the bookstands. I read most of them with considerable interest. Of course, they were extremely informative. But, there was something amiss. Though Dr Kalam has been regarded as a lover of children, none of these books were written specifically for children.

I began to feel an urge to narrate the achievements and greatness of Dr Kalam to children, by writing a book. But I was faced with a dilemma. Writing a book for children seemed a preposterous idea. So far, my writings have been in the form of news reports about aviation and space issues in my capacity as the Special Correspondent for *The Times of India.*

But still I decided to take my thoughts further. As a first step, I decided to assess children's interest and curiosity about Dr Kalam. I began to talk to my daughter Rimanika and her classmates about Dr Kalam. Despite their young age, they showed a tremendous interest in him, his role in making rockets and space flight in general.

Appropriately, the idea began to take on a serious shape when my wife, Usha and I were buying books from our friend, Mrs Saloochana Gulati, who promotes books for children. Her collection included several biographies on scientists written for children, but we spotted none on Dr Kalam. I casually mentioned this to Saloochana and she suggested that I write one.

There is yet another reason. I am a space buff and I have always envied those sitting in a mission control room, monitoring the flight of a rocket. Since that did not work out, I chose to take up a career in aerospace writing. This choice has given me a chance to meet many men of science and also visit important research centres. Ever since the eighties I have had a few opportunities to meet and interact with Dr Kalam. These occasions helped me in knowing the man at close quarters so that when I began this biography, a recall of those meetings provided valuable inputs in my work. Still, while writing this book I had to frequently refer to *Wings of Fire*, Dr Kalam's autobiography, and also to two of his other books *India 2020*, and *Ignited Minds* and Raj Chengappa's *Weapons of Peace.*

I am indebted to the following for sparing their valuable time to recall their association with Dr Kalam : former Chairman of Indian Space Research Organisation, K. Kasturirangan, its present Chairman, G. Madhavan Nair, former Director of the Satish Dhawan Space Centre, Sriharikota, R. Aravamudan, former Director of the Vikram Sarabhai

Space Centre, Vasant Gowarikar, former Director Light Combat Aircraft project, Kota Harinarayana, Director Nehru Science Centre, G. Rautela, Ms. Kavita Gadgil of the Abhijit Air Safety Foundation, V. Shankar of the South Indian Education Society, S. Suryanarayan of Aerospace Engineering department at Mumbai IIT.

I am thankful to the following institutions for providing references of pictures for rendering the illustrations in the book. Indian Space Research Organisation, Bangalore, Vikram Sarabhai Space Centre, Thiruvananthapuram, MIT– Aerospace Engineering, Chennai, Tata Institute of Fundamental Research, Mumbai, Nehru Science Centre, Mumbai, Dr Anil N. Suchak, Mumbai, Janmabhoomi Press, Mumbai and Anandalaya High School, Anand.

As it is my first attempt at writing a book, I acknowledge the tremendous help given by the staff of Navneet Publications. Thanks to my father, R.K. Laxman, who finally agreed to do the cover design for the book despite his poor health; my mother, Kamala, Usha and of course my daughter Rimanika, for providing me the encouragement.

Mumbai
26th January, 2004

(Srinivas Laxman)

CONTENTS

DO YOU HAVE TEN MINUTES FOR OUR COUNTRY?

Dr A.P.J. Abdul Kalam

Have you got 10 minutes for your country?
If yes, then read.

YOU say that our government is inefficient. YOU say that our laws are too old. YOU say that the municipality does not pick up the garbage. YOU say that the phones don't work, the railways are a joke, the airline is the worst in the world, and mails never reach their destination. YOU say that our country has been fed to the dogs and is the absolute pits. YOU say, say and say. What do YOU do about it?

We sit back wanting to be pampered and expect the government to do everything for us whilst our contribution is totally negative. We expect the government to clean up but we are not going to stop chucking garbage all over the place, nor are we going to stop to pick up a stray piece of paper and throw it in the bin. We expect the railways to provide clean bathrooms but we are not going to learn the proper use of bathrooms. We want Indian Airlines and Air-India to provide the best of food and toiletries but we are not going to stop pilfering at the least opportunity. Our excuse? It's the whole system which has to change.

So who's going to change the system? What does a system consist of? Very conveniently for us it consists of our neighbours, other households, other cities, other communities and the government. But definitely not me and YOU. When it comes to us actually making a positive contribution to the system, we lock ourselves along with our families into a safe cocoon and look into the distance at countries far away and wait for a Mr. Clean to come along and work miracles for us with a majestic sweep of his hand.

Dear Indians, this disgust is highly thought-provoking and calls for a great deal of introspection. It also pricks one's conscience, too.

I am reminding you of what John F. Kennedy exhorted to his countrymen, "Ask not what your country can do for you. Ask what you can do for your country."

This ten minute message from the First Citizen of India inspired us to bring out this life sketch for our young readers. It is our hope that in the finest hour of their lives they will be inspired by Dr Kalam's evergreen inspirational message and "Dream, dream, dream. Dream transforms into thoughts. Thoughts result into action."

"I miss my parents at this moment and I am deeply grateful to my teachers. They (children) can also treat their mother, father and school teachers as their role models."

1 EARLY DAYS

It was evening in the picturesque seaside town of Rameswaram, on the southern edge of Tamil Nadu. A cool breeze was gently blowing in from the sea. Along with the sound of waves lapping against the shore, could be heard the sweet sound of birds circling overhead.

Among the children playing on the beach was a boy with wavy hair and dreamy eyes. This youngster was Avul Pakir Jainulabdeen Abdul Kalam who later became the 11th President of India.

While spending time with his friends, Abdul was attracted by the sound of the birds flying above. He carefully observed as a fledgeling perched on a boat was trying to take off. It spread its wings, fluttered briefly and sprang up. The air seemed to give the needed thrust for its take-off! The bird soared up into the sky. It steered its pace and course with great ease. How Abdul wished he could fly like those beauties in the air!

This passion for flying, aroused by the beautiful birds, years later inspired Abdul Kalam to design India's first rocket which successfully placed a satellite *Rohini*, into orbit on July 18, 1980. It was called the SLV-3 (Satellite Launch Vehicle). At the time when Abdul was growing up, no one had even dreamt of such a happening.

Dr Kalam's house on Mosque Street, Rameswaram

Rameswaram, where Abdul was born on October 15, 1931, was a small town having narrow streets lined with old houses made of limestone and brick. The town was famous for its Shiva Temple. The temple consists of a long corridor of 213 metres, lined with statues of donors. Nowadays, people from all over the country visit his ancestral house on Mosque Street. Built during the middle of the nineteenth century, it is a small, simple bungalow which at one time had a blue exterior and a red-tiled roof. In the front there is a verandah where the family used to sit and chat, usually after dinner. The main room has a few items of furniture, a cupboard and a cot. In a corner, there is a shelf of books stacked with English and Tamil classics. Abdul stayed in that house with his father, mother, brothers and sister and led a secure and happy childhood.

Kalam's father, Jainulabdeen

Abdul's father, Jainulabdeen was a pious man. He led an austere life without depriving his family of the basic comforts. Abdul recalls his father getting up early in the morning and doing *namaz*. Near Abdul's house there was a mosque where his family prayed. Often people of different religions approached his father to seek his blessings. People would come to him carrying bowls of water. He would dip his finger in each of them and say a prayer. They then carried the water home to give it to the sick in their families, as a cure. After recovering from their illness, many of them visited Abdul's father at his home and thanked him. Sometimes, they even offered sweets as a token of their gratitude.

In this close-knit family, dinner time was always special. During this meal they exchanged views on a variety of topics ranging from family matters to spiritual subjects. During one such session Abdul asked his father about the significance of offering prayers. His father replied that when one prays the body becomes a part of the Cosmos, which knows no division of wealth, age, caste or creed.

The words left a profound impression on Abdul.

Rameswaram is believed to have been built on the very spot where Lord Rama placed his feet. During the annual Shri Sita-Rama Kalyanam ceremony the town becomes a centre of pilgrimage. The main income for Abdul's family was from ferrying the pilgrims across the sea between Rameswaram and Dhanushkhodi. Pilgrims visiting Rameswaram made it a point to visit Dhanushkhodi, 20 kilometres away in the sea. It is believed that Lord Rama bathed here and thus sanctified the place. The boulders between Dhanushkhodi and Sri Lanka are believed to be the remnants of the bridge used by Lord Rama to cross over to Lanka, the kingdom of Ravana in the epic *Ramayana*.

The Shiva Temple at Rameswaram

Ferrying pilgrims fetched good money and the family lived comfortably. But a devastating cyclone lashed the shores of Rameswaram and destroyed their boat. The family lost their only source of livelihood in one swift, tragic stroke.

Young Abdul wanted to help the family through the crisis. He realised there was a demand for tamarind seeds. He decided he would collect and sell them to a shop near his house. His family wanted him to concentrate on his studies. He said he would study as well as help his family. Reluctantly, everyone agreed. Even while studying or enjoying the evenings with his friends on the beach, he set aside some time to collect the seeds and sell them to the nearby shop. For this he was paid the princely sum of one anna !

Besides selling tamarind seeds, he helped his cousin Samsuddin sell the popular Tamil newspaper *Dinamani* to earn a little more money. At dawn several bundles of the newspaper, printed in Madras (Chennai), were thrown onto the platform of Rameswaram railway station from passing trains. Trains did not stop at Rameswaram station during those days of the World War II, as almost all of them were commandeered to transport troops.

Abdul, after picking up the bundles marked for his area, rushed and handed them over to Samsuddin. He gave Abdul a small amount for the service he had rendered. There was a great demand for *Dinamani* because the people wanted to know about India's freedom struggle and the latest developments of the War.

Thus did Abdul earn his first wages. However, it was the joy of being able to care for his family that Abdul cherished most. Even

decades later, he would recall with immense pleasure and a sense of pride, the incident of earning his own money for the first time, and the implications that this had, for him.

Newspaper bundles on the station platform

2 AT SCHOOL

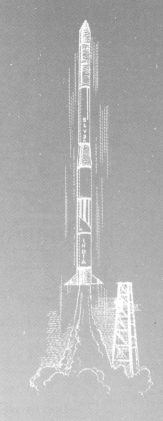

It was barely dawn at Rameswaram, but the Kalam household was already astir. Even the children had woken up and were rubbing the sleep off their eyes. Young Abdul had to hurry. He had just enough time for a quick wash before going for Arabic classes followed by a Mathematics tuition class where his teacher always waited in readiness for this eager pupil. After tuition, it was the practice for the children at his home, to have a mid-morning meal. Then, it was time for school, along a cobbled road.

Abdul first went to Rameswaram Elementary School. It was a simple building with a row of classrooms, no different from the classrooms of most of today's schools. Even as a child Abdul had an inquisitive mind which made him eager to learn about everything. English, Mathematics, Science and Tamil, were his favourite subjects.

In a letter to 12-year-old Jesal Shah, who had written to him after he became the President of India, Kalam described how different the schooling system was in his days. He said he carried only a few books to school. There was no schoolbag, no water bottle and no lunchbox. Daily he studied till 10.30 p.m. in between enjoying dinner with his family. He did his homework under the light of a kerosene lamp.

16

S.T.R. Manickam's house

After dinner Abdul would spend some time reading books he had borrowed from a freedom fighter, S.T.R. Manickam, who used to run a home library. Manickam's house was located on one of the main roads of Rameswaram. He spoke to Abdul about the importance of the *Bhagwad Gita* and the *Holy Koran*. Manickam later recalled that Abdul's favourite books included *My Experiments with Truth*, Mahatma Gandhi's autobiography, and Pandit Jawaharlal Nehru's *Glimpses of World History*. In 1997, Dr. Kalam wrote a letter to the man who had inspired him to read. "Your library was, in my youth, a source of great inspiration to me." He also presented Manickam with a book titled *100 Great Lives*.

What was Manickam's reaction to this gesture ? "I wish there was a book called 101 Great Lives because it would have a chapter describing the life of my dear young friend Abdul."

S.T.R. Manickam passed away in December 2002, at the age of 84.

At school, Abdul made friends easily. One of his closest friends was Ramanadha Sastry, the son of Pakshi Lakshmana Sastry, who was the high priest of the Rameswaram Temple. Ramanadha and Abdul shared the same bench in the class and were inseparable. The only apparent difference was their dress. Abdul wore a cap, the traditional headgear of a Muslim boy, whereas Ramanadha wore the local Brahmin attire.

One day a new teacher came to their class. While teaching, his eye fell on the pair sitting side by side. Being extremely conservative he could not accept the fact that a Muslim boy should be seated next to Ramanadha. He ordered Abdul to go and sit in the back row.

Abdul lifted his books and got ready to move to the back row. As he looked at Ramanadha through the corner of his eye, he found his friend on the verge of tears. The humiliation and agony was too much for them.

On reaching their homes that evening, both Abdul and Ramanadha narrated the unpleasant incident to their parents. That very evening Ramanadha's father summoned the teacher and told him in no uncertain terms that what he had done would only spoil the minds of innocent children and breed a sense of discrimination. The teacher was given an ultimatum – either he apologises or he leaves the school and the town of Rameswaram itself. The stunned teacher readily apologised. He had learnt a lesson in communal harmony for life.

Pakshi Lakshmana Sastry

This incident had left such a deep scar on Dr. Kalam's mind that in November 1997, when the Bharat Ratna was conferred on him, he told the media : "Even today I am living with the image imprinted on my subconscious mind of Ramanadha crying in the class when I changed to the rear row."

Unlike the new teacher, Sivasubramania Iyer, Abdul's science teacher, was a very broad-minded person. One day he invited Abdul to have lunch with him at his home. Iyer's wife was horrified at the idea of a Muslim boy eating in her kitchen ! She displayed her resentment by refusing to serve her young guest. Unperturbed, the teacher himself served the food to Abdul, while his conservative wife kept watching from behind the kitchen door !

The meal over, Iyer invited Abdul to lunch, the next weekend. Abdul initially hesitated. But Iyer explained to his pupil that change of any sort would always be accompanied by obstacles which had to be overcome with determination. Iyer's plan worked. During the second visit to his teacher's place, Abdul was struck by the difference. The teacher's wife had become warm and friendly. She led him to the kitchen and served him lunch herself! Abdul felt very happy. His teacher's persistence had succeeded in converting his wife into a broad-minded person.

Over lunch, Iyer expressed his wish that he wanted Abdul to be on par with the highly educated people of the big cities. Abdul was just fifteen then. Still, he thought over his teacher's words. One day at dinner Abdul told his family about his desire to go to a high school. The nearest one was in Ramanathapuram, the district headquarters.

His father's reaction to this suggestion reassured him. He said that he knew very well that his son would have to go away to grow.

Abdul felt happy that he was not being tied down to one place. He knew the change to a new school in a town would do him good. He was enrolled at the Schwartz High School, a boarding institution at Ramanathapuram.

Schwartz High School

Schwartz High School was known for the quality-education it imparted to the students. Moreover, the school put great stress on inculcating values in their minds. As a constant reminder to the impressionable minds, a plaque at the entrance had these words inscribed on it : "Let not thy winged days be spent in vain. When once gone, no gold can buy them back again."

Abdul's cousin, Samsuddin and his brother-in-law, Ahmed Jallaluddin, escorted him in a train to Ramanathapuram. Initially, Abdul felt very homesick for his family, his friends and his mother's delicious *poli,* made of plain wheat flour with coconut and sugar filling.

Gradually, he started enjoying the atmosphere of his new school. The teachers liked him and were appreciative of his work. Among those who exercised a lot of influence on him was Iyyadurai Solomon. A slightly balding man, Solomon always had a smiling face. The students thoroughly enjoyed his class because of his warm and friendly attitude and his frankness. His best advice to Abdul was that in order to succeed in life and achieve results one must understand and master three mighty forces – *desire, belief* and *expectation.* The teacher boosted the morale of the students by encouraging them to develop confidence and optimism.

**Kalam's teacher,
Iyyadurai Solomon**

While most of the teachers were popular with the students there was one who was a terror. He was Ramakrishna Iyer, the mathematics teacher. Generally, he wore a white turban, white shirt and tie. One day Abdul absent-mindedly wandered into a classroom where Ramakrishna Iyer was teaching. This annoyed him. The disciplinarian teacher refused to listen to Abdul's excuses and in front of the whole class the teacher caned him.

Months passed. The strict teacher held a mathematics test. When the results were announced Abdul was happy to have scored well in the

Ramakrishna Iyer,
the Mathematics teacher

test. This made Iyer very happy. Speaking to the students during the morning assembly session he proudly announced that whomsoever he caned became a great man and that Abdul was going to bring glory to his school and to his teachers. Abdul and Iyer became good friends after that and Abdul kept in touch with Ramakrishna Iyer even after he left school.

On the day he was sworn in as the President of India, there was a mood of excitement in the school. Sweets were distributed among the teachers and students. During the assembly, the teachers spoke to the students about the achievements of their former student, Abdul Kalam and asked them to emulate his example. Over the years, Iyer's prophecy has come true and the alumnus of Schwartz, Dr A.P.J. Abdul Kalam, has become a role model for India's youngsters.

"Henceforth I intend to share with them, my experiences, helping them to ignite their imagination and preparing them to work for a developed India for which the road map is already available."

3 ABDUL GOES TO COLLEGE

Abdul left Schwartz High School in 1950 as a determined and confident young man. As he stepped out of the school, the teachers blessed and assured him that one day he would reach the stars.

At that time the nearest college was St Joseph's College, in Tiruchchirappalli, 53 km away from Ramanathapuram, and Abdul decided to join it. This college offered many courses in science.

After examining various options, Kalam decided to study physics. His professors were Chinna Durai and Krishnamurthy. The strong impact that he had made on his teachers during his years in the college was evident in July 2002 when Kalam addressed the students and teachers of his alma mater. Prof. Chinna Durai, then in his nineties, had travelled over 160 kilometres from another town to Tiruchchirappalli to bless his former student. This gesture moved Kalam to tears.

There were other teachers like Prof. Thothathri Iyengar and Suryanarayana Sastry who taught him Mathematics. They were not unduly concerned that he did not obtain outstanding grades in the tests, because he was an all-rounder, possessing a good knowledge of the subject. This ability allowed him to understand things without much difficulty.

His teachers included Rev. Father R.N. Sequeira who taught English. Through his interesting lectures, this able guru succeeded in stimulating an interest in classics of literature among his students. This made Abdul read the works of famous writers like Leo Tolstoy, Walter Scott, Thomas Hardy and the like, during his spare time. Whenever possible, Abdul would make a dash to the library where he would pick up volumes, flip through the pages and borrow some of them.

Father Sequeira was the hostel warden. Kalam often recalled how Father Sequeira would visit each of the 100 hostel inmates every night, carrying a Bible in his hand. He would exchange a word or two with the students, enquire about their welfare, attend to their individual needs and do his utmost to make the youngsters feel at home.

At the hostel, which became a home away from home for the students, Deepavali was a day which they would always remember. On this day, Father Sequeira arranged for the boys to have the traditional oil bath. The students enjoyed this session very much because Father Sequeira introduced a competition to see who finished the bath first and emerged from their toilet well oiled.

When Kalam was in the third year, he was made the secretary of the vegetarian mess. On a Sunday afternoon, they invited the college rector, Rev. Father Kalathil, for lunch. The students had made numerous preparations reflecting their individual tastes. Father Kalathil enjoyed all the dishes and congratulated them on their efforts.

Kalam spent four years in the college and got his B.Sc degree. But, by this time he had come to realise that the study of Physics did not particularly excite or thrill him. He began to think about switching over to Engineering and constantly debated with himself about the career path he should follow. He remembered his childhood when he was fascinated by the mysteries of the sky and the flight of the birds.

He came to the conclusion that aeronautics fascinated him because it symbolised freedom. There was another incident which inspired him to study aeronautical engineering. As a boy, when he was distributing newspapers at Rameswaram, he had read an article about British war planes. He went through the article a number of times. Building and flying planes had by then developed into a burning desire in him.

Then came another question. Where should he apply ? He got the details of various institutes. Finally, he applied to the Madras Institute of Technology (MIT), which had one of the finest courses in various branches of engineering, in the country.

4 TAKES OFF TO MIT

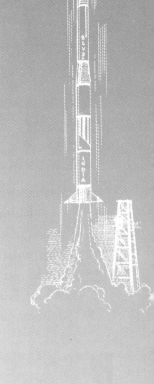

Kalam duly filled in the application form for entrance to the Madras Institute of Technology (MIT). But, he still felt uncertain about getting admission. While submitting his application he was aware that he was trying his luck with one of the top engineering institutions in the country.

Meanwhile, he continued to pray hard. And one afternoon when the postman knocked at his door he found that his prayers had been answered. Here was the letter from the MIT saying that he had got admission. Kalam was thrilled, excited and happy.

The family was eager that he should join the institute, but his father could not afford it. They were in a fix because of the huge amount involved in doing the course. There were intense discussions as to how they would be able to help Abdul get enrolled in the institute. They did not want to deprive him of a good education. As they explored various possibilities, Abdul's sister, Zohara realising how disappointed her brother would be if he did not get into MIT, decided to mortgage her gold bangles and chain to raise the money. It was her act of generosity which really placed Abdul in the aeronautical orbit. So grateful was he to her that he vowed then and there to release the pawned jewellery

AERONAUTICAL ENGINEERING

The study of aeronautical engineering enables students to apply the ideas of science and technology for making, maintaining and flying aircraft, rockets, missiles and satellites.

It is a technically-advanced, challenging and exciting area of work because an aeronautical engineer will one day see the plane, or rocket, or missile, or satellite, which he or she has designed, fly. Those best suited to study aeronautical engineering are students who like to face challenges and arrive at quick solutions to problems.

In India there are a number of institutes offering courses in aeronautical engineering.

the moment he started earning. And, he honoured his commitment.

Kalam joined the institute with a sense of anticipation. Classes and projects kept the students of the institute fairly busy. Kalam also fell in step with this hectic routine. Unlike the majority of his colleagues, he found an unusual way of spending his leisure hours at the institute. What really attracted him in the new environment were two old decommissioned planes which had been kept in the institute to facilitate

Madras Institute of Technology – Department of Aeronautical Engineering

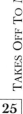

World War II plane – Kalam taking notes

demonstration classes. He could not take his eyes off the two vintage beauties. So fierce was his joyous energy to gain knowledge about flying that each day after class, Kalam would head straight towards the planes, instead of his hostel room, and observe them in detail.

He would carefully study each section – the wings, the propellers, the cockpit, the main body, the tail and the wheels and jot down his observations. To Kalam they were marvellous pieces of engineering and triggered in him a desire to design and operate planes. He decided that after completing his study of aeronautical engineering he would try to become a pilot and actually fly planes.

At the institute, four of his teachers interacted with him closely and moulded him. Professor Sponder, an Austrian national, taught aerodynamics which deals with the science of flight.

Prof. Sponder was a pleasant person, but expected his pupils to work hard and keep themselves updated about the latest developments in aeronautics. His advice to Kalam was, not to worry about future prospects; instead he felt, it was more important to lay sound foundations, to have sufficient enthusiasm and an accompanying passion for one's chosen field of study.

Prof. K.A.V. Pandalai took classes on the structure of an aircraft. Kalam remembered Prof. Pandalai as a cheerful, friendly and enthusiastic individual. Years later, at a meeting of the Aeronautical Society of India in Mumbai, Prof. Pandalai remembered his old student Kalam, with affection. He recalled that Kalam was hardworking and intelligent. "He was a bright youngster and I was confident that he would bloom one day," he said.

Prof. Narsingha Rao's method of teaching Mathematics was stringently meticulous. This habit rubbed off on his young charge to such an extent that in the years that followed, Kalam acquired the reputation of carrying a "surgical knife," to meetings where aircraft designs were reviewed. This means that Kalam would analyse and review, in considerable detail, every aspect of a plane under discussion, and put probing questions to the participants at the session.

Besides these three, there was Prof. Kurt Tank, a German national, who later joined Hindustan Aeronautics Limited. He had designed India's first multi-role fighter aircraft, the HF – 24 -1 *Marut*. This plane achieved fame during the 1971 Indo-Pak War.

HF-24 Marut

The HF-24 multi-role Marut aircraft was the first indigenous fighter aircraft made at the Hindustan Aeronautics Limited at Bangalore. It was designed by Dr Kurt Tank. The government was keen on building this aircraft to reduce its dependence on foreign countries for getting its military planes.

The construction of the fighter began in June 1957 and it flew for the first time on June 24, 1961. Its main features include a small swept wing, with two engines. It could operate at a maximum speed of 1128 kilometres per hour and had a flying range of 800 km indicating the distance it could travel without refuelling. It could fly at supersonic speeds when it reached a height of 40,000 feet. The pilots who flew this plane were happy with its performance as they could control its movement skilfully and easily.

A total of 147 HF-24s were manufactured and the plane made its mark during the 1971 Indo-Pak War. The aircraft served the Indian Air Force till 1985 after which it was replaced by MiG-23 aircraft.

As part of the aeronautical engineering course, along with four of his classmates, Kalam was assigned to work on a project which involved designing an attack aircraft. He focussed mainly on the aerodynamic aspect of the plane, while his team concentrated on the aircraft's engines, its structure and instruments.

The five of them worked very hard but progress seemed slow. Unable to collect all the required data, Kalam's team was behind schedule by two weeks. On a Friday afternoon, Kalam was summoned by the institute's director, Prof Srinivasan, to his office.

Prof. Srinivasan said he had reviewed the progress of the project and found it disappointing that Kalam and his team could not submit their project on time. When Kalam tried to explain, the professor simply refused to listen to him. He was in no mood to entertain any excuses for not being able to complete the project within the specified period.

He then looked at Kalam and said: "Look young man, today is Friday. I will give you three days. If by Monday morning I do not get the drawing, your scholarship will be stopped." The words hit Kalam like a sledgehammer. If the scholarship were withdrawn it would be the end of his dream to fly ! Visibly shaken, he did not know what to do for a brief moment. After he regained his composure, he assured Prof. Srinivasan that he would do his best and complete the project by the following Monday.

Being a determined person with a positive outlook, Kalam took up the challenge of completing the project in 72 hours. He worked all through that Friday night even skipping dinner. He slogged throughout Saturday, his head bent over his drawing board, making calculations and refining the design of the aircraft. At that time, the outside world did not exist for him and nothing distracted him.

It was Sunday. There was the usual lazy mood in the campus. Most of the students were listening to

Kalam working on his project at MIT

music, reading, strolling around or enjoying a chat among themselves. But, not Kalam. He woke up early, refreshed himself and was back at the drawing board.

While he was at his job, Prof. Srinivasan watched him from a distance. He then moved closer to his pupil, patted him on the back and said: "I knew I was putting you under stress and asking you to meet an impossible deadline. I never expected you to perform so well under stress," he told Kalam. These words, after the harsh ones earlier, boosted the morale of Kalam and his brave band.

Despite all these challenges and the heavy schedule of projects and deadlines, Kalam's days at MIT had their lighter moments. He did not miss an opportunity to participate in the institute's extracurricular activities. He took part in an essay competition organised by the MIT's Tamil Sangham (literary section). His piece was called: *Let Us Make Our Own Aircraft*. He took a lot of trouble writing it. It was a subject very close to his heart. A few days later when the results were announced, it was Kalam's laudable effort that received the first prize from *Ananda Vikatan*, the highly popular Tamil weekly.

The winning of the prize seemed like a prediction of Kalam's future achievements. His choice of the subject was of considerable significance. In the years to follow, this prize winner was to play a major role in the design and development of the indigenous fighter aircraft which was developed after a gap of several years, the Light Combat Aircraft (LCA). As a major player in the designing and developing of this aircraft, Kalam seemed to have brought to fruition the concept that he had written about, in his college essay.

Kalam had completed his course successfully and the moment was nearing for him to bid farewell to the institute. As was customary the teachers and students posed for group photographs. Kalam was standing in the third row. Just before the cameraman was about to click, Prof. Sponder looked around for Kalam. He spotted him in the rear row. He wondered why his favourite pupil should be standing so far. He invited Kalam to sit with him in the front row with the teachers.

While this photograph was being taken Prof. Sponder told Kalam, "You are my best student. Hard work will help you to bring a great name for your teachers in future."

Kalam's life as a student had come to a glorious end and a new phase, involving planes and rockets, was about to begin.

On September 4, 1998 while inaugurating the golden jubilee celebrations of MIT, Kalam took the opportunity to revisit his alma mater. He spoke fondly of the faculty and said with humility that he owed the greatness of his achievements to the influence of his teachers. He repeatedly emphasised that it was a joy for him to study at the MIT.

LIGHT COMBAT AIRCRAFT

The Indian Light Combat Aircraft (LCA) was designed and developed at the Aeronautical Development Agency at Bangalore. It was assembled at the Hindustan Aeronautics Limited, also in Bangalore. Its chief designer is Dr Kota Harinarayana, an expert in aircraft designs.

LCA is a small plane with a single-seat and single engine. It is light and is an all-weather multirole supersonic fighter.

The LCA had its first flight on January 4, 2001 at Bangalore. With this flight India joined the group of nations which have the capability to design supersonic military aircraft.

5 HINDUSTAN AERONAUTICS – A STEP AHEAD

When Kalam left the MIT, there was a feeling of satisfaction and fulfilment in him. He had obtained a diploma in aeronautical engineering. Now he wanted to utilise his knowledge and work on actual aircraft. He came to know that there were openings in this line, at the Hindustan Aeronautics Limited (HAL), in Bangalore. He applied for a job there.

How happy he felt when he got the good news that he had been chosen as a trainee at HAL! After all he loved planes. And he had landed safely at a place where aircraft were made.

The HAL establishment consists of a huge factory located close to Bangalore airport. Most jets for India's defence forces are manufactured here. The beginnings of this sprawling establishment can be traced to the year 1940 when a famous industrialist, Walchand Hirachand, set up a company jointly, with what was then the government of Mysore, to manufacture aircraft.

Over the years HAL underwent several organisational changes. Each change marked a step further in its development. It set up units in different parts of the country and by the end of the 1990s, HAL had manufactured over 3000 planes of 20 different types. About 95 per cent of them were for the Indian Air Force (IAF).

These ranged from combat aircraft to trainer aircraft and transport planes for carrying men and material to the far-flung borders of India.

During his first few days at HAL, Kalam went around looking at the planes with thrill and excitement. When he started hands-on work, he chose working on the shop-floor. He was assigned to a section where aircraft engines were being overhauled. He found putting his theoretical knowledge to practical use exciting and challenging.

As he learnt at his job, he got acquainted with other aspects of aircraft engine systems. Many of the HAL staff who taught him were experienced men who had learnt their job through hands-on assignments. Thanks to their practical approach of imparting knowledge, Kalam was able to learn things very fast. That is why he always enjoyed every opportunity he had to enter into serious discussions with them, on aircraft. His interactions with them also had an enlightening aside. He not only acquired a deep knowledge about the working of an aircraft but also understood the need for a close relationship between man and machine. These lessons of interdependence between man and machine helped him to develop a meticulous approach.

Time flew and soon he had completed his training and become a graduate aeronautical engineer. He came to know that there were job openings in two places, both indeed very close to his dream of flying. One was with the IAF (Indian Air Force) and the other with the Directorate of Technical Development and Production [DTD&P (Air)]. The latter department, which is attached to the Defence Ministry, provides on-the-ground support to planes used by the IAF.

Kalam decided to try his chance with both these openings and sent in his applications. He was pleasantly surprised when both the employers asked him to appear for interviews. He was of course keen on joining the IAF since it would enable him to fulfil his childhood dream of flying. At the same time he felt that the job at the DTD&P (Air) would give him the chance to manage the actual operation and maintenance of flying machines.

IAF held its interview at Dehra Dun, while the DTD&P (Air) screened its applicants at New Delhi. He had to travel 2000 km to appear for the interview at New Delhi where he performed satisfactorily. After this, Kalam went to Dehra Dun for the Air Force interview. He was feeling both nervous and excited. When the results of the IAF interview were announced he found he had stood ninth among the 25 candidates who had been interviewed. The first eight were chosen. Kalam had not made it.

Even though he had earlier on reasoned with himself that either of the two openings would satisfy him, he felt a crushing sense of defeat after the IAF results. He wanted to seek solace and advice from someone he could talk to. He felt Swami Sivananda at Rishikesh would be the best person.

Kalam meets Sri Sadguru Swami Sivananda at the Divine Life Society Ashram at Rishikesh

A LONGING THAT CONTINUES

Kalam's longing to join the IAF still lingers, it seems. When in August 2003 Kavita Gadgil, the mother of late Flt Lt Abhijit Gadgil, a MiG-21 pilot who was killed in a crash, met him, Kalam relived that incident. She says, "He talked of how he wanted to fly planes. He narrated how disappointed he was when he found that he was 9th in the list of eligible candidates, but only eight were taken. When my husband pointed out that he was the Supreme Commander of all the military air power, he responded with a disarming candour to say, 'But it's not the same thing as being a pilot'."

From Dehra Dun Kalam trekked down to Rishikesh to meet the Swamiji. The weather was chilly. At a distance he could see the snow-clad mountains of the mighty Himalayan range. On the way he bathed in the Ganga. Reaching Rishikesh, he went straight to the ashram and was ushered into the presence of the Swamiji.

There Kalam immediately felt a sense of calm. The Swamiji seemed to have guessed Kalam's plight. Urging him to speak, the Swamiji listened intently as Kalam told him about the cause of his dejection. Kalam repeatedly explained that his dream had always been to fly like a bird some day.

The Swamiji advised him to accept his destiny and go ahead with his life. He added that what one was destined to become was pre-determined. The words seemed to convey a definite message. Kalam thanked the Swamiji and returned to New Delhi.

When Kalam went to the Ministry of Defence, he was informed that he had been chosen as a Senior Scientific Assistant on a salary of Rs 250 per month. Kalam sent his acceptance of the offer. One of his earliest assignments was to design an aircraft which could fly faster than sound.

When he finished his project, Kalam was shifted to the Aircraft and Armament Testing Unit (A&ATU), at Kanpur to carry out studies for a fighter aircraft christened *Gnat*. He also received an exposure to aircraft maintenance practices. Kalam learnt of the way planes are serviced periodically. The work also included changing damaged and worn-out parts of the aircraft.

GNAT AIRCRAFT

The *Gnat* aircraft was first manufactured and flown in the UK in 1955. It was designed by the famous aeronautical engineer W.E.W. Teddy Potter. He and his team of designers had aimed at designing a plane which was small and yet would perform satisfactorily.

In 1958 *Gnat* joined the fleet of the Indian Air Force and proved its worth during the 1965 Indo-Pak War. So impressed was India with these aircraft that subsequently Hindustan Aeronautics Limited (HAL) started manufacturing them.

The first *Gnat* was assembled at HAL on November 18, 1959 and was called *Ajeet*. It was a single engine aircraft which could attain a maximum speed of 1080 kilometres per hour.

Once the *Gnat* became airworthy, Kalam was due for a change again. He came back to New Delhi and was assigned to various aircraft projects. He enjoyed these assignments and enriched himself by the varied experiences.

When he finished three years in the department, he realised that the time had come for him to change jobs once again. He looked around for options in the field of aerospace development. Luckily, the government had set up a new aerospace unit at Bangalore called the Aeronautical Development Establishment (ADE). Kalam was happy to get his orders to join the unit.

The Gnat Aircraft

> *"For indigenous development, technology denial from the developed world came as a book for us to develop technologies."*

6 AT THE ADE

Kalam was his usual spirited self once again and excitedly looked forward to working at the Aeronautical Development Establishment (ADE), in Bangalore.

This aeronautical establishment was set up in 1959. It focussed on aerospace research work to assist the IAF. In the 1970s and 1980s, its role expanded when different facilities were added, including a flight simulator. A flight simulator is a ground-training device which represents as well as reproduces exactly the conditions experienced on the flight deck of an aircraft. Trainee pilots learn to fly, using a flight simulator. Apart from designing and developing a flight simulator, the scientists at the ADE had also developed a remotely piloted vehicle for carrying out surveys from the air with the help of a camera. It could be used over different terrain. Its movements could be controlled by operators sitting on the ground.

Kalam joined the ADE at this time. For the first few months, he was not assigned any specific project. He occupied himself in observing the different types of research and development work being done, particularly in the field of aeronautics. Dr O.P. Mediratta, the Director of the establishment, kept a careful watch on the new recruits. Among them, one received his special attention and that was

Kalam. The more the Director watched Kalam the surer he became of the new recruit's potential. Dr O.P. Mediratta decided to assign to him a difficult job. He was asked to lead a team of scientists for making a heavier-than-air flying machine, called a hovercraft and launch the engineering model in three years.

The project was an entirely new concept in India and for a moment Kalam did not know how he would go about designing and developing it. But, being a true scientist, always keen to explore and develop new discoveries, he decided to take up the challenge. He and his group were fired with enthusiasm for yet another reason. Their hovercraft would be a purely Indian product built without any foreign assistance. Moreover, a hovercraft has some relation to the field of aeronautics as well. For instance, this vehicle can fly a few feet above the ground on a cushion of air blown from under it. The advantage of such a vehicle for battlefield operations is that it can easily travel over different kinds of surfaces – mud, water and marshes. The ADE felt the hovercraft would be a boon to our Armed Forces as it would enable them to move across any type of flat surface, including water.

As a first step the project-team began a search of scientific information on hovercraft. Being a new concept, not much data was available about it even in technical magazines. One person who came to their rescue, at last, was Prof. Satish Dhawan. Prof. Dhawan was in the Faculty of Aeronautics at the Indian Institute of Science, Bangalore. He taught Kalam and his associates how to design a propeller for the hovercraft by holding five classes for the team.

HOVERCRAFT

A hovercraft is a vehicle which is suspended upon a cushion of air. This cushion is generated by a fan attached to the engine of the hovercraft. The hovercraft control is through the use of rudders, like the type used in planes. The advantage of a hovercraft is that it can fly over relatively flat surfaces of land, snow, mud, water, swamp and rivers. Currently, they are being increasingly used for ferrying passengers and also troops during war. There are different types of hovercraft, made in various parts of the world. Some years ago there was a hovercraft service linking Mumbai with Navi Mumbai and it proved extremely popular. But, it had to be discontinued for a variety of reasons. There is a proposal to restart the service once a new airport is constructed at Kopar, in Navi Mumbai.

V.K. Krishna Menon and Kalam with other scientists

Admittedly, these lessons were a help. But information about its other technical aspects continued to draw a blank. Despite this disadvantage, the group, under the leadership of Kalam, went ahead with the project. The vehicle started taking shape in the ADE's workshop.

Among those who wholeheartedly backed the project was V.K. Krishna Menon, then the Defence Minister. Menon felt that the project marked the beginning of self-reliance for the country. Since a number of defence-related laboratories were located at Bangalore, Krishna Menon often visited the city to review their functioning. During one such visit, the minister expressed a desire to travel by the hovercraft which had been christened *Nandi*, the bull mount of Lord Shiva.

The people at the ADE were looking forward to the demonstration also. It was still an unproven vehicle and some scientists wondered whether it would be safe for the minister to travel by it. A sense of apprehension prevailed on the day of the demonstration.

As the Defence Minister climbed into the hovercraft the scientists waved to him and wished him a pleasant journey. Just as it was about to start, an IAF officer, who was accompanying the Defence Minister, offered to fly the machine saying it would be dangerous if it was operated by an 'inexperienced' person like Kalam. The atmosphere turned tense. But Krishna Menon brushed aside this suggestion. Kalam gladly took the captain's seat. This incident really boosted his morale.

The minister apparently enjoyed the journey. When he returned he even suggested that a more powerful vehicle should be produced. The hovercraft project was a complete success. Among those who had watched Kalam fly the hovercraft was his well-wisher and 'teacher' Dr Dhawan, who was loud in his congratulations. He patted his 'student' vigorously as if to say 'well done.'

The successful trial run of the hovercraft became well known in scientific circles. A number of scientists and engineers visited the ADE, travelled in it and evaluated its performance. They included Dr M.G.K. Menon who was then the Director of the Tata Institute of Fundamental Research (TIFR) in Mumbai. His ride lasted 10 minutes. When he disembarked, he made routine enquiries about Kalam and the project, and left.

TATA INSTITUTE OF FUNDAMENTAL RESEARCH

The Tata Institute of Fundamental Research (TIFR) was founded by the father of India's nuclear programme, Dr Homi Bhabha who wanted to further the cause of science in India. In 1943, Dr Bhabha approached the famous industrialist, J.R.D. Tata and requested his support for setting up the institution.

Tata very enthusiastically agreed and in June 1945 the institution began functioning under the leadership of Dr Bhabha at the campus of the Indian Institute of Science in Bangalore. Six years later, it moved to Mumbai and functioned from a bungalow called *Kenilworth,* on Gopalrao Deshmukh Marg (Pedder Road), where Dr Bhabha was born. The bungalow has since been demolished and in its place a residential apartment block also called *Kenilworth* was constructed for the officers of the Department of Atomic Energy.

Ten years later, the TIFR shifted to its present sprawling campus at Colaba. It was inaugurated by former Prime Minister Jawaharlal Nehru on January 15, 1962. Over the years it has carried out research in the areas of astronomy, astrophysics, mathematics and nuclear physics to name some of the key areas.

Dr Homi Bhabha

J.R.D. Tata

Tata Institute of Fundamental Research (old and new premises)

Though the hovercraft project was dropped after Krishna Menon's resignation it proved to be a launching pad for Kalam's career in space. A week after Dr M.G.K. Menon had travelled in the hovercraft, Kalam received a call from the Indian Committee for Space Research (INCOSPAR), to attend an interview for the post of a rocket engineer.

Kalam could not believe it. This offer was a windfall for the young scientist. There had been no formal application for this post by Kalam. It was obvious that Dr Menon had played a role in it. A mere 10-minute ride in a hovercraft was now launching Kalam into space.

All these years Kalam had heard and read so much about the TIFR where INCOSPAR was based, and now he stood right in front of it. Its sleek structure, the well tended lawn with the murmur of the sea in the backdrop, impressed him. Yes, he was at the very institute which is regarded as the cradle of India's space programme.

When he told the official at the reception desk the purpose of his visit, he was ushered into a room where Vikram Sarabhai, often referred to as the father of India's space programme, Menon and Saraf, of the Department of Atomic Energy, were already seated. They greeted him in a friendly manner. The interview was pleasant and informal.

After the interview was over, he was requested to remain in Mumbai for a few days. The next evening when he was visiting the TIFR, he was informed that he had been selected for the post of rocket engineer. He thanked God. As a rocket engineer, he would be working on the development of rockets and dealing with space flights. Finally, he was getting closer to his cherished dream.

> *"I will meet with a large number of young students and narrate the beautiful events which took place in aviation, from the Wright Brothers to Thumba."*

7 AT THUMBA

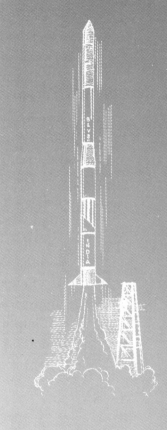

After a brief Familiarisation Course at TIFR Computer Centre at Mumbai, Kalam, along with a team of scientists, left for Kerala, in the latter half of 1962 on another exciting mission. They were chosen by INCOSPAR to set up the Equatorial Rocket Launching Station at Thumba, a place not far from the state capital Thiruvananthapuram.

Thumba then was a quiet fishing village. At that time, to an ordinary person, Thumba's only attraction seemed to be its picturesque scenery, its unspoilt beach dotted with coconut trees. Its most prominent landmark was a medieval church named after St. Mary Magdalene.

This fishing village is very close to the earth's magnetic equator, which is an imaginary line round the earth where the magnetic needle remains horizontal. It had caught the attention of scientists Dr Vikram Sarabhai and Dr Homi Bhabha. To these two famous scientists, Thumba seemed the ideal spot for launching rockets as there were no disturbances around.

Besides the scientific advantages, materials and equipment could easily be transported from Thiruvananthapuram to Thumba. Scientists from all over the world could fly into the capital and then take a short 20-minute drive to Thumba, to watch and carry out rocket launches. So Kalam and his team got down to work at this ideal space station with a great deal of enthusiasm.

But to acquire 600 acres of land for the space station would involve relocating its inhabitants elsewhere, as human habitation cannot exist too close to a sensitive space testing outfit. To add to the problem, within the selected area was the Church of St. Mary Magdalene where the people and local Christian community worshipped.

The space scientists working with Kalam felt uncertain about the villagers' reaction. Some scientists even felt they had hooked their hopes on an impossible star.

But, the scientists were in for a pleasant surprise. On a Sunday morning the Bishop of Thiruvananthapuram, the Right Reverend Dr Peter Bernard Pereira arrived at Thumba. Addressing the congregation at the beautiful church, he explained to the fishermen the importance of space technology and the significance of India launching its own space flights. He was a keen supporter of the Indian space programme.

The Church of St. Mary
Magdalene at Thumba

He further said that the country's space scientists wanted Thumba as they felt it was the right spot geographically, to launch rockets. What would be their message to him? Would they agree to leave the area and shift to another place?

The villagers debated among themselves. Their answer was like a soft rumble and then came a loud reply in a chorus, "Amen!" The fishermen of Thumba had set their seal of approval on India's space programme, with a prayer on their lips.

The sound echoed through the walls of the church. Many at Thumba, said it was an auspicious start. The fishermen in a backward zone had played a key role in launching India into a hi-tech space era.

In due course the formalities of acquiring land was completed. Immediately, Kalam and his colleagues began the job of setting up the complex. The church housed the first office of the Thumba Space Centre. The prayer room was converted into Kalam's laboratory and the Bishop's house, an

43

The Bishop's House, Thumba

annexe of the main church, was the team's design and drawing office. Currently, this church houses the Indian Space Museum.

One day when Kalam was at his desk in the church, he received an unexpected telephone call from a top official from the Department of Space. When he spoke to the official, he gave Kalam the good news. He had been chosen by Dr Vikram Sarabhai to go to the US for a six-month training course on Sounding Rockets at the National Aeronautics and Space Administration (NASA), along with some other Indian space scientists.

Prior to his departure, he went to Rameswaram to spend a few days with his family. Everyone at home was proud of the fact that he had been selected for the NASA programme. There were emotional scenes on the day he left for Mumbai to catch his flight for New York. His parents blessed him and his friends asked him to write to them as often as he could. His brother-in-law Jallaluddin, and his cousin, Samsuddin, the duo who had escorted him to high school years ago, now came with him to Mumbai to see him off at the Santa Cruz airport.

At first Kalam was attached to NASA's Langley Research Centre (LRC) in Virginia. Established in 1917, it is in the forefront of research in the field of aeronautics and space technology. After he had worked here for some time Kalam moved to NASA's Goddard Space Flight Centre at Greenbelt, Maryland, near Washington. At this Centre, he familiarised himself mainly with satellites having scientific applications. Finally, his training programme took him to NASA's Wallops Flight Test Facility at Wallops Island in Virginia, where he studied about sounding rockets.

While he enjoyed his training at all the NASA facilities, he particularly remembered, the one at the Wallops Flight Test Centre. The sight of sounding rockets thundering skywards was not the only attraction. The entrance to the space complex left a deep impression on Kalam. There was a painting of a battle scene, the armies using conventional weapons as well as rockets. He found, to his pleasant surprise, that it had glorified the achievements of Indian rocketry. It showed Tipu Sultan's army fighting the British soldiers with rockets. Kalam was happy this historic memorabilia had been carefully preserved at the Wallops Centre.

The painting was also the last thing he saw each day on his way to his lodgings at a hostel near the Wallops Facility, together with R. Aravamudan, a fellow scientist from India. The two would dine at a self-service cafeteria on mashed potatoes, boiled beans or peas, bread and milk. During the weekends they would take a flight to Washington in an old Dakota plane, which was a service offered by NASA. The room rent at Washington had been reduced for NASA officials to six dollars for an overnight stay. While in Washington they made it a point never to miss the latest film being screened and visit a supermarket mainly for buying presents for their families and friends.

The Indian group returned to Thiruvananthapuram in mid-1963. Meanwhile, the rocket centre at Thumba had seen a few changes. France, the US and Russia, had begun to take an interest in the scientific work being done there. For Kalam too, Thumba appeared different, since they were coming back from a well-equipped space centre in the US to a new one at Thumba, it felt like working on an assembly kit, after one has been handling a very sophisticated piece of digital equipment.

Even their accommodation at Thiruvananthapuram was in an uncomfortable hotel in the heart of the city. Food too, was a problem as it was not easily available at odd hours. These scientists who often worked late, on their return from Thumba would find the food counters at the hotel shuttered and the kitchen washed clean for the night.

To their surprise they discovered that the only place where dinner was available at that hour was the Thiruvananthapuram railway station. From their hotel it was a 10-minute walk to the railway station through a meandering narrow lane. At the station's cafeteria which was always crowded, they had to queue for their breakfast which consisted of idlis and sambhar. Since there were no eating places at Thumba or even anywhere near it, the scientists collected packed idlis and puris from the railway cafeteria for lunch.

Then they would have to wait for quite some time at a bus stop outside the railway station for a Kerala State Road Transport Corporation (KSRTC) bus to take them to Thumba. The fare for the one-hour long journey was just 90 paise. At Thumba, those days the only way the scientists could move from one end of the Thumba centre to another was either by walking or cycling. Reliving those times, Dr Aravamudan, Kalam's colleague and fellow scientist recalled, "Since the (motor) van was always busy, Dr Kalam who was not a cyclist, would hitch a ride with me. In those days, even rocket parts and payloads were transported by bicycle."

They had a hectic five-day week at Thumba either supervising the construction of different facilities like the launch pad, laboratories and workshops or designing a rocket. They worked so hard that they never looked at their watches, sweating it out in the

A part of a Sounding Rocket being transported on a bicycle

A Sounding Rocket on the launch pad at Thumba

humid weather. Therefore, the arrival of the weekend was eagerly awaited. Usually on Saturdays and Sundays, they visited Kovalam or Shankumukham and enjoyed whiling away their time on the beach. Since Kalam enjoyed swimming he would plunge into the sea at the first opportunity.

"By the late 1960s our office rented a beautiful old building called *Ingledine* opposite the Thiruvananthapuram Raj Bhavan and converted it into a club, with two badminton courts, a table tennis table and room for card players. Dr Kalam was an enthusiastic badminton player," recalled his colleague.

Thumba meanwhile was developing into a full-fledged rocket launching complex and came to be known as the Thumba Equatorial Rocket Launching Station (TERLS), with a launch pad, a mission control centre and various other buildings. While the construction and development activity of Thumba got going, scientists started preparations for the launch of the first sounding rocket.

During those days at Thumba, Kalam had the important job of integrating the different parts of the rocket and making sure of the safety operations. His colleague D. Easwardas was in charge of assembling and launch, while R. Aravamudan was entrusted with radar, telemetry and ground control. The rocket was assembled in the church and taken to the launch pad in a truck.

SOUNDING ROCKETS

These rockets are used for atmospheric studies. They carry payloads of different weights to altitudes ranging from 48 kilometres to 1,287 kilometres. They are low cost rockets and allow scientists to conduct investigations at a specified time and place. Their flight time is usually less than 30 minutes.

After a sounding rocket is launched, the payload, which carries out the studies, detaches itself from the main body of the rocket. This happens when the rocket motor has used up its propellents. The payload then continues to fly into space and begins conducting atmospheric experiments. When the experiments are completed, the payload begins to re-enter the atmosphere. At this point a parachute is deployed which ensures that the payload touches land smoothly.

As yet the team had not built a sounding rocket of their own. An American sounding rocket supplied by NASA was to be launched from the newly-built launch pad at Thumba. The model arrived piecemeal from NASA. It belonged to the Nike-Apache class of rockets, presumably named after the great North American tribe of Apache Indians.

Its flight was fixed for the evening of November 21, 1963. While it was being positioned on the launcher by a manually-operated crane, a minor technical problem occurred in the crane. As the launch time – 6.00 p.m. – was nearing, the scientists manually lifted the rocket with their own hands and placed it on the launch pad.

Exactly at 6.25 p.m. the rocket lifted off with a bang. A few minutes after it had taken off, it started relaying information about the performance of the rocket itself as well as the atmosphere. The mission was successful. The mood among the scientists changed from suspense and nervousness, into jubilation. They congratulated each other and thumped each other on the back.

The experience the scientists had gained with the launch of the Nike-Apache sounding rocket gave them enough confidence to develop sounding rockets within the country itself. They then started designing a series of rockets called *Rohini*. Over the years, several hundreds of these rockets have been launched, mainly from Thumba. These rockets have also been used for carrying out studies about the weather. The development of these rockets eventually led to India making its own rockets for launching satellites into orbit.

A total of 3,198 sounding rockets have been so far launched from Thumba. Of them, 1,847 were made in India.

> *"In spite of the denial of critical technology from the developed countries India's missile pro-gra-mme is on course and at no time it was rattled due to technology control regimes. Every government has supported it and the march is on."*

8 SLV–3

Dr Vikram Sarabhai's agenda after the work done at TERLS, took on a visionary turn. He then concentrated on the development of an Indian satellite launch vehicle. This was the outcome of his firm belief that a strong, indigenous base in science and technology would benefit the nation. Dr Sarabhai, who gave the go-ahead for building a satellite launch vehicle, foresaw that it would serve as a testing tool for future rocket development.

In plain terms a satellite launch vehicle (SLV) can place a satellite in orbit. The first one made in India was a four-stage rocket meant to place a 40-kilogramme satellite, called *Rohini,* in orbit. Its flight was considered important because it would be the first time that India would place a satellite in orbit.

The SLV project that Dr Sarabhai had envisaged, was a challenging one and to implement it called for a good team. For this historic Indian space mission, Dr Sarabhai had decided upon a team based on the professional background and personal traits of its members.

The team brought forth four design options (configurations) for the SLV. Dr Sarabhai selected the third option and thus the vehicle came to be called SLV-3. SLV-3 was a four-stage satellite launch vehicle. The team was further divided into four groups. Each of these

49

groups was entrusted with developing one stage of the four-stage rocket. Kalam and his team were asked to design the fourth stage, that is, the upper stage rocket, which would give the final velocity to put *Rohini* in orbit.

Dr Sarabhai deputed separate project leaders for each of the four stages. The scientists chosen were V.R. Gowarikar, A.E. Muthunayagam, M.R. Kurup and Abdul Kalam, all of them brilliant men of science.

Dr Sarabhai provided the needed impetus to the team. According to Kalam, the very announcement "Sarabhai coming" energized everyone whenever this scientist used to visit Thumba to hold meetings with them.

During the day Dr Sarabhai spent his time mainly discussing administrative issues. He never got tired and was full of energy and enthusiasm. At night, when the day's routine work was done, he would convene a meeting of the SLV project engineers. These meetings were usually marked by heated arguments about technical details. Seeing Dr Sarabhai's style of work, Kalam always believed that the idea of making SLV rockets was born at night.

Kalam discussing with Dr Sarabhai the SLV Project

Dr Sarabhai was convinced that Kalam would enjoy the support of his colleagues as well as be a good leader. Dr Sarabhai had once met Kalam along with an Air Force official V.S. Narayanan, at the Ashoka Hotel in New Delhi, to discuss an important military project. During this meeting Dr Sarabhai had realised that Kalam had the makings of a visionary leader.

With the rocket steadily moving from drawing board to the workshops, the Thumba Space Centre began to attract a large number of visitors from the global science fraternity. Among them was Prof. Hubert Curien, who headed the French space organisation, Centre Nationale de Etudes Spatiales (CNES).

On the day of Prof. Curien's visit Dr Sarabhai asked Kalam to give a presentation about the fourth stage of SLV-3 to the visiting team. After the presentation it was mentioned that the fourth stage of SLV-3 was also being considered as the upper stage for the French satellite vehicle *Diamont P-4*. A decision was taken that SLV-3 fourth stage should be reconfigured to suit both vehicles.

But in 1971, the French government cancelled the *Diamont* order when it was ready and about to be delivered. There was another major shock to follow in the same year. Their mentor, Dr Vikram Sarabhai passed away in Thiruvananthapuram, following a heart attack, on December 30, 1971.

The whole complex at Thumba was renamed Vikram Sarabhai Space Centre (VSSC), to honour Dr Vikram Sarabhai, the father of India's space technology. In 1972 the government appointed Dr Satish Dhawan as Chairman of ISRO in addition to his position as Director of the Indian Institute of Science, Bangalore, and Dr Brahm Prakash, the country's foremost metallurgist, was appointed the first Director of VSSC.

Dr Dhawan decided to have a single project director for the entire SLV-3 mega project and the man he chose was Abdul Kalam. Kalam had initially developed payloads for sounding rockets. Although he was neither the seniormost nor did he have a doctoral degree, Kalam had two essential attributes in his favour. He was creative and he was a team man, "a welder of people", as the media called him.

As Project Manager for developing the SLV-3, Kalam had to shoulder new responsibilities. As the team leader, he succeeded in forging great unity in the group. Several scientists willingly co-operated. His boss Dr Brahm Prakash and other senior scientists noticed how well the SLV team was being led. But Dr Brahm Prakash's words of praise were mingled with caution. He told Kalam during a meeting: "The SLV mission will be accomplished with, and through, a large number of people. You will require a tremendous amount of tolerance and patience." Such golden words, of course, broadened his vision. Still his work routine went on with the rigour and regimen required by the projects.

Kalam's day would begin with an early morning walk around the lodge he was staying in at Thiruvananthapuram. While taking his stroll, he would plan his day. On reaching his office at Thumba, he would clean his desk himself and arrange the papers related to SLV-3 according to their priority. Then, he held a meeting with his team members and set the targets for the day. These brainstorming sessions were always enlightening and congenial.

Yet the project did not always run smoothly. Kalam wanted 275 engineers and scientists to work on it but he could get only 50 people, as

The SLV-3 Team : A member making a presentation

the rest were needed in other departments. Despite limitations the group made satisfactory progress. Each member had specialised in a particular field of rocketry and their collective knowledge made important contributions to the SLV mission.

While executing each stage Kalam stressed upon his team members the importance of core factors. These were the capability to design the rocket, setting goals and above all, the ability to withstand failures. He jotted down individual suggestions and provided handwritten notes to his colleagues, asking them to implement short-term plans that could be completed within five or ten days.

Around this time, Kalam suffered severe personal losses. His brother-in-law, Ahmed Jallaluddin died in 1974. Two years later his parents passed away. No doubt these tragedies had a shattering effect on Kalam. But he did not allow them to come in the way of his work or affect the progress of the SLV-3 project. "To succeed in your mission, you must have a single-minded devotion to your work," he repeated to himself. He had nothing else on his mind except the flight of SLV-3. This meant cutting down his time for relaxation like reading, or playing his favourite piece of classical music *Endaro Mahanubhavulu,* on the veena, or writing poetry in Tamil.

Gradually as the hardware began emerging from the drawing boards, everyone was charged up. Some put in 40 hours a week, while some others never looked at their watches and worked from anything between 60 to 100 hours a week, sometimes even during weekends, sacrificing the time they could have spent with their families. Those at home never grumbled because they knew that the scientists were involved in an important space project which was a national mission.

By the time the fourth stage of SLV-3 was developed and tested, a new requirement came up. India was building a small communication satellite APPLE (Ariane Passenger Payload Experiment), to be launched by the European Ariane Launch Vehicle. The SLV-3 fourth stage was included in the payload of the Ariane Launch, as it was a perfect fit. APPLE was placed in geostationary orbit and communications with earth stations started. This achievement boosted the morale of rocket technologists of India and was a fulfilment of Dr Sarabhai's vision.

Kalam and Prof. Satish Dhawan, Chairman of ISRO

Prof. Satish Dhawan and Dr Brahm Prakash at one of the SLV-3 review meetings

In 1976, Dr Brahm Prakash on returning from France after successfully testing the SLV-3 rocket motor, informed Kalam that Wernher von Braun, the great rocket scientist, was to visit Thumba. Kalam had often recalled the setbacks that had bogged the work of Wernher von Braun — the man who had played a major role in the mission which had placed Neil Armstrong and Edwin Aldrin on the moon. When Kalam heard the announcement by Dr Brahm Prakash, he was eager to meet the man.

Rocket scientist Wernher von Braun

WERNHER VON BRAUN

Wernher von Braun was born on March 23, 1912, in Germany. He was one of the world's first and foremost rocket engineers and a leading authority on space travel. His interest in space began when his mother presented him a telescope with which he started studying the stars, planets and the moon. Another factor which triggered in him an interest in space was Hermann Oberth's book *Rocket Into Planetary Space.* His natural leadership and his ability to inspire and encourage others, motivated him at the age of 16 to organise an observatory team. He also enrolled himself at the Berlin Institute of Technology in 1930 and two years later, at the age of 20, he received a degree in mechanical engineering.

His determination to expand man's knowledge through the exploration of space motivated him to develop a series of rockets and satellites. Some of the rockets are the *Jupiter, Pershing, Redstone* and the famous *Saturn* which took man to the moon. He was also involved with the world's first space station called the *Skylab*.

During the Second World War, von Braun and his team developed powerful rockets called *V-2*. These wrought havoc over London and other parts of the United Kingdom.

When the Second World War ended, von Braun led about 500 German scientists through war-torn Germany to surrender to the Americans in a secret operation code-named *'Operation Paperclip.'* Once he reached the shores of the US, he dreamt of a world in which rockets would be used for peaceful purposes. Thanks to von Braun's efforts, NASA launched seven Apollo missions to the moon from 1969 to 1972.

Imagine Kalam's delight when he was deputed to receive von Braun at Chennai airport and accompany him to Thumba !

Seconds seemed to stretch into minutes as Kalam eagerly waited for von Braun's aircraft to touch down. The rocket experts warmly greeted each other before boarding the Avro aircraft during the ninety-minute flight to Thiruvananthapuram. Von Braun showed a keen interest in the SLV-3 mission. Kalam found him very humble and extremely soft-spoken.

Everything about the Indian space centre interested von Braun and he put a lot of questions to his escort. When he saw the SLV-3 taking shape, he remarked that it was a genuine thoroughbred, Indian in design and effort. He echoed Dr Sarabhai's words when he said that if Indian scientists wanted to do anything of significance in rocketry they should do it themselves. Citing his own earlier disappointments and setbacks, he remarked, "You should always remember that we don't just build on successes, we also build on failures."

During the few days that the duo spent together, they exchanged views on a number of subjects. When the topic turned to rocketry, von Braun emphasised the need for hard work, total commitment towards the project by the scientists and engineers, and above all their complete involvement with the mission. "Do not make rocketry your profession, your livelihood – make it your religion, your mission."

How deeply embedded were these words in Kalam's mind ! After ten years of total commitment, India's SLV-3 dream was about to be realised with the first experimental launch scheduled for August 10, 1979.

> *"I see many challenges and opportunities in front of us for the coming decades. Young scientists and aviators have a great role to play in building up futuristic aerospace technologies."*

9 SUCCESS AT SHAR

Simultaneous with the development of the SLV-3, work was on, for the development of a suitable launch site. Sriharikota, on the east coast was zeroed upon, as a suitable choice.

A three-hour drive from Chennai takes one to Sullurpetta, a dusty, chaotic and dirty wayside town. But a little later one realises there is something special about this place. Talk to any child on the roads of this town and they will reel out the names of different rockets and satellites, both Indian and foreign. Sullurpetta is the last township before one reaches India's main spaceport, Sriharikota.

The drive to Sullurpetta skirts the Pulicat Lake known for its pelicans. From a distance a bare outline of different types of structures, mainly water tanks and a huge tower, begin to come into sight. Soon one is greeted by different Indian rocket models dotting a traffic island of greenery, demarcating the entrance road into the spaceport of Sriharikota, which has been renamed as the Satish Dhawan Space Centre after the famed space scientist. This Centre can justly be called India's gateway to the moon and planets.

The history of this huge spaceport began in early 1968 with Dr Vikram Sarabhai wanting India to build and launch its own rockets and satellites to reduce chances of vested interests exerting influence on our scientific plans and developments. Keeping this in mind he wanted India to have her own rocket launching facility.

In 1968 the Andhra Pradesh government had offered the Space Department land free of cost at Sriharikota which was at that time a jungle filled with deadly snakes, scorpions and other reptiles. The area was occupied by a tribal population called Yanadis. Dr Sarabhai undertook an aerial survey of the place and gave the go-ahead for acquiring the land and making it a full-fledged rocket launching centre. The Yanadis, like the fishermen of Thumba, willingly handed over the area to the Space Department.

Sriharikota, 80 km north of Chennai and 13° north of the equator, has an area of 12,141 hectares with a 20-kilometre-long coastline. Coincidentally, it was in 1969, when NASA was planning its first manned mission to the moon that the work on converting Sriharikota into a spaceport began. Two and a half years later, on October 9, 1971, the first sounding rocket was launched from the spaceport at Sriharikota.

Over the years Sriharikota has blossomed into a well-equipped spaceport with several facilities. It is also an excellent combination of the ancient and the modern. The place abounds in Siva Lingas and more than 200-year-old temples to Lord Vishnu. Some of the Lingas have now been preserved in the garden of the Brahm Prakash Block which is the administrative centre of Sriharikota. The space centre is therefore not only a mecca for spacebuffs, but also gives solace to those who have a

LOCATION OF THE SPACE CENTRES

The reason why the space centres in India have been built on the eastern part of the country is that a rocket can take advantage of the earth's west to east rotation, during a launch. The rocket gets an additional push when the spaceport is in the eastern part of the globe, during its lift-off into space. This explains why NASA's Kennedy Space Centre and the European Space Agency's launch centre at Kourou, in French Guiana are located on the eastern coast. Secondly, the spent stages of the launches can fall off into the sea, with less damage to life or property.

religious bent of mind. It is a rare spaceport where the awesome thunder of zooming rockets mingles with the melodious clanging of temple bells.

The development of Sriharikota did not diminish the importance of Thumba. This space station continued to be the launch centre for the *Rohini* sounding rockets. Other powerful rockets for placing satellites in orbit, are launched from Sriharikota. These powerful rockets are brought piecemeal from the Vikram Sarabhai Space Centre at Veli, near Thiruvananthapuram by road to Sriharikota escorted by a high security team.

On arrival this special "parcel" of rocketry is assembled together and readied for a launch from the Sriharikota launching pad. From this moment, it is indeed hard work for the space team. Scientists have to assemble it inside a huge structure known as the mobile service tower. Prior to the much awaited lift-off the mobile service tower, weighing 3,200 tonnes, is shifted to its parking lot a little distance away from the launch pad. This tower has 32 wheels in each corner and moves on a rail track. The scientists and engineers work round-the-clock inside this tower. The final act of carefully placing the satellite on the topmost portion of the rocket is undoubtedly the most important part of their assignment.

During the days preceding a take-off, the mission control centres are a beehive of activity, with the scientists monitoring various parameters of the rocket on their computers. The crucial task of integrating the various stages of the rocket and fuelling the rocket, is also controlled from here. No wonder the scientists on the project can barely snatch a few hours of sleep during this time.

A day or two before the take-off, the scientists meet to decide whether the rocket is ready for the launch. If all of them give a go-ahead signal for the mission, the rocket blasts off on the specified day, to the thunderous applause of the hundreds of people, including a huge contingent of media persons, who would have assembled on the terraces of the buildings in Sriharikota. If the scientists detect even the slightest suspicion of trouble they give a 'hold' signal to the launch. The Mission Control Centre handles the actual take off of the mighty rocket till the satellite is placed in orbit. This operation usually takes about twenty minutes. Thereafter the spacecraft control centre at Bangalore takes over control in the case of remote sensing satellites, while the centre at Hassan (Karnataka) takes over control in the case of communication satellite launched by the GSLV. The Mission Control Centre is linked to all ground stations. At the spaceport there are also facilities to track the flight of the rocket.

The word, 'go' was abuzz at Sriharikota, with the much awaited first flight of the SLV-3 rocket in place. As it was a major scientific step forward in the Indian space programme, people were eagerly waiting to hear the news of the mission.

The launch date was fixed for August 10, 1979. In preparation for that historic day the mighty four-stage, 23-metre long, 17-tonne rocket stood on the launch pad. The previous evening at sunset it was silhouetted against the orange twilight sky bathed in the brilliant glow of arc lamps, positioned close to the launch pad. Visitors had already started arriving at the site for a grandstand view of the rocket's take-off. The townspeople of Sullurpetta had much to talk about and discuss those days as a rocket of this calibre was a special sight even for their eyes.

Amidst all this activity, Kalam had rarely left the mission control room, located a few kilometres away from the launch pad. This room is the nerve-centre of the flight mission during launches. It consists of several computers giving information about different aspects of the rocket and minute details about the flight. The scientists sit in front of the computers monitoring the data. There is also the countdown clock that flashes the time left for the lift-off.

In this room there is also a special enclosure for visitors which is usually packed to capacity during a launch date. Though the scientists have to sit glued to their computers, the visitors have a comparatively easier time. They can watch the scientists at work as well as look out of the adjacent balcony and actually watch the rocket take off. Because of the tremendous noise that the rocket makes during this time, some of the visitors close their ears, pucker their noses and squint, during the exciting moments. The blast off is so loud that it is known to have caused minor cracks in the windows of the glass-panelled mission control room.

On the day of the SLV-3 launch Kalam, being the Mission Director, was in the computer room much before any visitor had come in. From the early hours of the day, along with his colleagues he was monitoring the countdown. He was satisfied. All the computers indicated a 'go' signal for the electronic launch.

As is customary, ten minutes before any launch the computer takes over control of the rocket's flight. At Sriharikota Range, too, the computer had begun its task. The scientists who had so far been manning the operation had become spectators, watching their computers at work. The countdown clock was flashing 20 seconds and counting down; 15 seconds 14-13-12-11-10-9-8. At 8 seconds left for the lift-off, the computer flashed a warning that the rocket should not be launched because of a technical problem.

Kalam and his scientists wondered what had gone wrong as everything had seemed okay till that moment. They studied the data in the computer and found that there was a hitch. He hurriedly summoned his colleagues and held an emergency meeting. Should they, or should they not go ahead with the launch ? The team came to the conclusion that the problem was a minor one and that they could afford to ignore it. Though Kalam was in charge he accepted their joint decision. Launch it, was his verdict.

Exactly at 7.58 a.m., there was a rumble and the ground shook. Many standing in the visitors' gallery waiting to see the rocket lift-off, began to put their hands to their ears. Below them the scientists were already showing signs of elation. They envisaged their manufactured marvel streaking across the blue sky and going higher and higher.

The SLV rose majestically from the launch pad. The splendid lift-off triggered an enthusiastic applause from the onlookers. Scientists and engineers exchanged congratulatory handshakes and embraced each other. The rocket rose higher. Its first stage performed perfectly. The scientists began to breathe easy. Everyone felt delighted.

But this mood of elation and expectation was soon changed into terrible disappointment. When the second stage got activated, the rocket went out of control and it began to tumble. The flight had to be terminated 317 seconds after its launch. The vehicle's remains, with the payload, splashed into the Bay of Bengal, 560 km off Sriharikota.

A post-flight review found that the first launch of SLV-3 had failed because of a flaw with the second stage control system. A solenoid valve controlling the flow of red fuming nitric acid (RFNA) to one of the thrusters failed to close and the nitric acid had leaked away. With the thrusters unable to function without nitric acid, the vehicle went out of control and fell into the sea.

Immediately the news of the failed launch flashed on TV screens as Mission Director Kalam took all the blame. The failure came as a tremendous blow because years of hard work had come to naught in those few seconds.

Kalam was quite frustrated and physically exhausted. He headed straight for his living quarters, slumped on his bed and fell into a deep sleep. Late in the afternoon a gentle touch on the shoulder woke him up. It was his friend and mentor Dr Brahm Prakash. Guessing the sense of despair in Kalam, Brahm Prakash took him for lunch to take his mind off SLV-3.

A group of journalists who had come to Sriharikota to witness the launch were now waiting to talk to Kalam. Dr Dhawan in the spirit of a true friend, requested him to attend the meeting along with him. He offered to answer all the questions that the journalists would pose and give them satisfactory answers. True to his word, Dr Dhawan gave the journalists convincing answers to their queries. He ended the session by confidently declaring that the failed mission was not the end of satellite flights. There would soon be the next one and this time, it would succeed! Kalam felt a bit cheered after this. In time, others too, added their support to Kalam and his team. Among those who gave him moral support during this difficult time was Dr Brahm Prakash. He repeatedly assured Kalam that the entire scientific community was standing by him and urged him to continue with preparations for the next flight.

Soon preparations were in full swing for the second flight. By this time the team had recovered from their earlier disappointment. Kalam told himself that sometimes scientists had to wait for years to see their dreams turn into reality. Such thoughts exerted positive influences on Kalam's mind.

So when July 18, 1980 dawned at Sriharikota, there wasn't anything apparently different. By mid-morning, however the scene had changed. Scores of cars speeded ahead on the road to Sriharikota. They crossed the Pulicat Lake where the shores were alive with groups of pelicans basking in the sunshine. As the aquatic and terrestrial delights gave way to the familiar sight of rocket structures, the mobile service tower and the water tanks of Sullurpetta, the visitors knew that they were coming closer to their destination.

Bathed in the morning light the SLV-3 rocket was a spectator's delight. Enclosed on top of the rocket was the *Rohini* satellite. Unlike the excitement of the previous time, there was an air of nervous expectancy among the hundreds of scientists and engineers. The countdown was on, and everyone was praying for the success of this flight.

At 8.03 a.m. the rocket's engines ignited. A second later the rocket, with the *Rohini* satellite, gracefully lifted off from the launch pad. As it gathered speed every second, it formed an unforgettable sight against the blue morning sky over the spaceport. Birds flew off in all directions as the air reverberated with the thunder of the rocket zooming skywards.

Six hundred and two seconds after lift-off, precisely at 8.15 a.m., Kalam made the

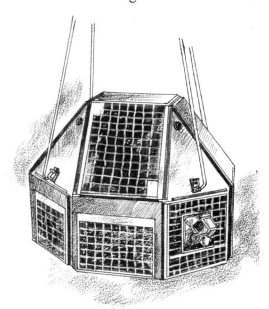

Rohini satellite

most significant declaration in his life. "Mission Director calling all stations. Stand by for an important announcement. All stages performed to mission requirements." The fourth stage apogee motor had given the required thrust to put *Rohini* satellite into orbit. In plain speak, the flight had been a thundering success.

On hearing the much-awaited announcement, the atmosphere at SHAR and at VSSC became instantly festive. People clapped and exchanged congratulatory handshakes and embraces. Some of the scientists broke into that classic song of camaraderie, *"For he's a Jolly Good Fellow"*, in honour of their beloved team leader.

The whole nation was electrified by this cent per cent indigenous effort, which made India one of the few countries capable of launching

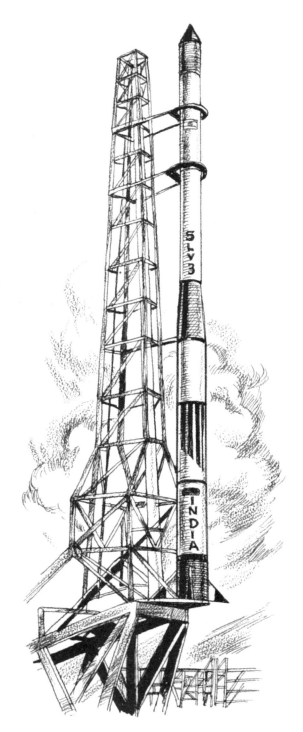

SLV-3 on the launch pad

a satellite. Earlier, Japan had suffered four successive failures before putting their first satellite in orbit, in 1970. Kalam and Dr Gowarikar (who had taken over as Director of VSSC, when Dr Brahm Prakash had retired in November 1979), were mobbed at the Thiruvananthapuram airport. The media went overboard in praise. Newspapers carried banner headlines; radio and TV aired special programmes. The Lok Sabha and Rajya Sabha MPs greeted the news with the thumping of desks. An elated Prime Minister Indira Gandhi, cabled her congratulations. In the 1981 Republic Day honours the President conferred a Padma Vibhushan on Dr Dhawan and a Padma Bhushan on Abdul Kalam.

**Kalam receiving the Padma Bhushan from
Dr Neelam Sanjeeva Reddy**

With the success of the flight, Kalam became internationally famous, with newspapers in India and abroad carrying photographs of him. He was described as one of the foremost rocket scientists in the world. In his hour of triumph Kalam remembered Dr Sarabhai and other earlier 'giants' of the space programme, the hundreds of personnel at VSSC and especially Dr Satish Dhawan and Dr Brahm Prakash, who had successfully guided the project.

Among the organisations which invited Kalam to speak was the Nehru Science Centre in Mumbai. An enthusiastic audience inspired him to give a detailed presentation about the SLV-3 mission. When the meeting ended he was besieged by autograph hunters. While still obliging them by signing autographs he was informed that there was a telephone call for him. It was from the Chairman of the Indian Science Research Organisation, Dr Satish Dhawan. He asked Kalam to take the very next flight to Delhi because the Prime Minister, Indira Gandhi, wanted to congratulate him personally.

For a moment he was a little hesitant. The reason? He felt he did not have proper clothes for such an occasion. He was not wearing a jacket and tie. His feet were shod in sandals.

He mentioned his dilemma to Dr Dhawan, who, as usual, gave him a patient hearing. Then came the spontaneous reply which merits a place in any book of quotable quotes : "You are beautifully clothed in your success." Kalam's mind was made up.

The meeting was held at the Parliament House. Among the other members who were there to join in the congratulations Kalam saw a

Dr Satish Dhawan and Abdul Kalam with Prime Minister Indira Gandhi

familiar face. It was Dr M.G.K. Menon, who had been the first to spot his capabilities at the time when Kalam had piloted him around in the hovercraft at the Aeronautical Defence Establishment (ADE), in Bangalore, years ago.

On his return from Delhi, Kalam resumed his round of work as before. Though the SLV-3 mission had been a thundering success, Kalam felt a time had now come for him to hand over the important project to other scientists. He wanted to be relieved of the project and was succeeded by Ved Prakash Sandlas, for the SLV-3 Continuation Project which aimed at making operational satellite launch vehicles of a similar class. But Kalam still took a keen interest in its flight.

Meanwhile the upgradation of SLV-3 by means of certain technological changes led to the development of an Augmented Satellite Launch Vehicle (ASLV), which had a payload capability of 150 kg. Other satellite launch vehicles notably Polar Satellite Launch Vehicle (PSLV) and Geo-Synchronous Satellite Launch Vehicle (GSLV), were also being envisaged during this time. Erstwhile team members of the SLV-3 project were now heading these new developments. Kalam took up the position of Director, Aerospace Dynamics and Design Group, so that he could configure all these technological developments.

As part of SLV-3 Continuation Project, the next SLV-3 flight, SLV-3 D1 took off on May 31, 1981. In his new role of Director, Aerospace Dynamics and Design Group, Kalam watched it soar up, trail-blazing a beautiful plume of yellowish flame. He was seated in the visitors' gallery this time and clapped heartily along with the other guests, when the mission was finally declared a success.

The turning point in Kalam's career soon followed. In January 1981, he was invited to give a talk at the Defence Electronics Applications Laboratory (DEAL), in Dehra Dun. The subject of his talk was the SLV-3 mission. Among those who heard Kalam that day was the eminent nuclear scientist and Scientific Advisor to the Ministry of Defence, Dr Raja Ramanna. After the talk the two retired for a private meeting over a cup of tea. Dr Ramanna asked Kalam whether he would be interested in leading the country's Guided Missile Development Programme (GMDP) at the Hyderabad-based Defence Research and Development Laboratory (DRDL).

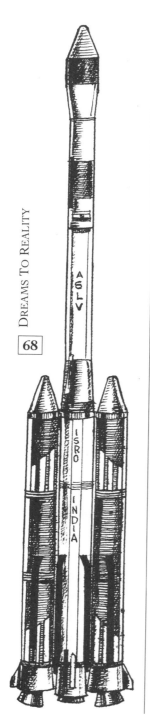

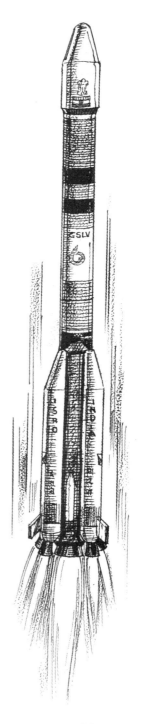

ASLV **PSLV** **GSLV**

Satellite Launch Vehicles

THE AUGMENTED SATELLITE LAUNCH VEHICLE (ASLV)

ASLV is a five-stage rocket meant to place in orbit a 150-kilogram satellite. The rocket's maiden flight in March 1987 from the Satish Dhawan Space Centre in Sriharikota was a failure because of a technical problem. The second one also failed because of a technical flaw. The third and fourth flights were successful. This was the Stretch Rohini Satellite Series (SROSS). These satellites were mainly experimental satellites.

THE POLAR SATELLITE LAUNCH VEHICLE (PSLV)

PSLV is a rocket consisting of four stages and its length was 44.4 metres. Its primary mission was to place in orbit a remote sensing satellite weighing between 1000 and 1200 kilograms.

So far there have been seven flights of the PSLV and to the credit of the Indian space community, except the first one, launched on September 20, 1993, all other flights were successful. Today, even foreign scientific missions use the PSLV to launch their satellites.

The importance of the PSLV lies in the fact that it will be used for India's moon mission slated for launch by 2008 and designated as *Chandrayaan-1.*

THE GEO-SYNCHRONOUS SATELLITE LAUNCH VEHICLE (GSLV)

GSLV is a three-stage rocket, 49 metres in length. At present the third stage of this rocket is powered by a Russian-made cryogenic engine but the Indian model is currently being developed.

This super rocket is used for placing in orbit nearly 2000-kilogram communication satellites for the INSAT (Indian National Satellite System) series in the geo-stationary orbit 36,000 kilometres above the equator. Currently, these satellites are being launched by an *Ariane* rocket from the European spaceport of Kourou, in French Guiana.

An advanced version of the GSLV is currently under development called GSLV Mark 3. At present both the PSLV and GSLV are meant for only one-time use. This means after launch, the rocket falls into the sea and cannot be used again. ISRO, therefore is seriously considering developing a reusable launch vehicle, which will place a satellite in orbit and land back, like an aircraft, on a regular runway. The advantage of this is that it will be cost-effective.

Once again Kalam was in a dilemma. Should he remain a part of ISRO and develop the next generation of rockets or should he help in the design and development of military rockets, (termed missiles), which would enhance national security? Well-known for his leadership qualities, both ISRO and DRDL were keen to avail of his services. The two organisations were pulling him with equal force towards their side. The tussle went on for over a year till a final decision was taken at the highest level with ISRO giving Kalam to DRDL.

On May 31, 1982, Kalam bade farewell to ISRO after 18 eventful years. By way of farewell, Prof. Dhawan asked him to give a talk on 'The Space Programme Profile in India by the year 2000.' It was attended by the entire ISRO management and staff. The roll of claps, at the end of this brilliant lecture echoed loud and long as Kalam, moved on ... ahead.

SATISH DHAWAN SPACE CENTRE

ISRO's launching Centre at Sriharikota (SHAR) was named the Satish Dhawan Space Centre after Prof. Satish Dhawan, the Chairman of ISRO from 1972 to 1984, which were its formative years. It was renamed on Teachers' Day September 5, 2002. Unveiling the plaque, the Prime Minister said that Prof. Satish Dhawan was a multi-faceted personality, truly, one of the most distinguished Indians of our times – a brilliant aeronautical engineer, an outstanding space scientist, a philosopher, a humanist, and above all, a great visionary. "His unique human qualities, combining intense personal charm with a deep commitment to social values and an extraordinary objectivity in management, led several generations of students, colleagues and administrators to efforts that, perhaps, would not have been undertaken otherwise," he noted and added that scrupulous objectivity and deep concern for society's problems always marked his leadership.

By naming this important space establishment Satish Dhawan Space Centre, the nation, has paid its humble tribute to Prof. Satish Dhawan, who epitomizes growth of science and technology and its implications to society and its overall progress. Prof. Dhawan was a teacher par excellence and India was paying its tribute to him, especially on Teachers' Day, by naming SHAR after him.

"There have been two major milestones in my life, the launching of the Rohini satellite from SLV3 vehicle in 1980... and flight test of the Intermediate Range Ballistic Missile, 'Agni', in 1989, from Interim Test Range in Orissa."

10 THE FLIGHT OF AGNI

On the first day of his new assignment as Director of DRDL on June 1, 1982, Kalam stepped into the defence laboratory in Hyderabad recalling the saying, 'Strength respects strength.' He reasoned that if India had potent weapons she would be respected by all nations. Kalam firmly believed that if India had to be on a par with the developed countries she would have to possess different types of missiles.

To this end he set about his work with a will. Within a short time, he had made his mark. As was his habit, Kalam went around familiarising himself with the establishment. On taking charge of the laboratory he found it largely staffed by disgruntled scientists. With his superb leadership qualities, Kalam succeeded in infusing a new sense of enthusiasm among them. He explained to them the importance of their project and convinced them that they would be playing an important role in national security.

Gradually, the terrible feeling of disgruntlement gave way to a new mood of enthusiasm. The scientists began to work for longer hours even during weekends to ensure the fruition of their prestigious project. The 'Kalam-magic' had rubbed off and endured.

Soon after his taking charge, a detailed study was carried out for evolving advanced

71

missile systems to counter the emerging threats to the security of India. Besides the scientists, experts and members of the Armed Forces took part in this study, and it culminated in the Integrated Guided Missile Development Programme (IGMDP) comprising the design, development and deployment of five indigenous missile systems.

The five missile projects were *Prithvi* (Earth) Surface-to-Surface missile, *Trishul* (the trident of Lord Shiva) Short Range Surface-to-Air Missile, *Nag* (Cobra) an Anti-Tank missile, *Akash* (Sky) Surface-to-Air missile and *Agni* (Fire) named by Kalam himself, an Intermediate Range Two-stage Ballistic missile.

The Defence Minister R. Venkataraman approved the programme and sanctioned an unprecedented budget of Rs. 388 crores for its speedy implementation. The IGMDP project was launched by Dr V.S. Arunachalam, Scientific Advisor to the Defence Minister on July 27, 1983.

Accomplishing this project was a big challenge because missile technology had been the monopoly of a few selected nations. Kalam had a formula for its successful outcome. It involved four basic factors — goal-setting, positive thinking, visualising and believing. Kalam's formula found immediate acceptance among his team colleagues. To meet the enhanced space requirement of IGMDP, a model high technology research centre with advanced technical facilities was set up in the nearby Imarat Kancha area and named Research Centre Imarat (RCI).

The next logical step for checkout of the missile systems was to look for a suitable site for missile flight trials. The choice fell on Chandipur in the Balasore district of Orissa. The name means the abode of the goddess, Chandi or Durga ! There was a beautiful bird sanctuary in Chandipur. Being an ardent nature lover, Kalam asked his engineers to design the test range without disturbing the sanctuary. Called the Interim Test Range (ITR), it was established in 1989.

While the test range at Chandipur was being built, the first launch of the missile programme was successfully conducted on September 16, 1985 when *Trishul* took off from the test range at Sriharikota. The successful launch raised the morale of the workforce by several degrees.

**The successful launch of *Prithvi*,
the surface-to-surface missile**

Prithvi was launched on February 25, 1988, an epoch-making event in the history of rocketry in the country. It is cent per cent indigenous with a range capability of 250 km with different types of payload and warheads, and was the first of the four missiles to be inducted into the Army. Moreover, it could be modified from a long range Surface-to-Air missile system and could also be deployed on a ship.

The realisation that India could do it, sent shock waves across some neighbouring countries and so angered the Western bloc that it clamped a technology embargo !

Undeterred by such impediments, the DRDL team of 500 scientists networking with many organisations went ahead with the huge effort of launching *Agni*. The launch was scheduled for April 20, 1989. Unlike a rocket launch, a missile launch involves wide-ranging safety

One of the cartoons in the *Times of India* after the failure of
the first two *Agni* launches

**Nothing to be discouraged! We have postponed it again
because we want to be absolutely certain!**

measures. People living in nearby villages were moved to safety. The countdown for the launch started 36 hours earlier. At 14 seconds before launch, the computer signalled 'Hold', indicating that a system was functioning erratically. In another few seconds, there were more 'Hold' signals. The first launch had to be aborted, to the team's utter dismay. The second launch ten days later, had also to be postponed for technical reasons. Kalam boosted the morale of his dejected colleagues by recounting his earlier SLV-3 failure. He asked them to be positive and remain confident. He assured them that the programme would succeed.

And it happened on the morning of May 22, 1989. The attention of not only India, but that of the whole world was focussed on Balasore. What is so significant about *Agni* that attracted the attention of the world? This missile having a range between 1,500 to 3,000 kilometres gives India a powerful punching power because it has the capability to launch a nuclear strike. Also, for the first time, scientists were able to try out what is known as a re-entry technology. This means that the warhead of this weapon, which strikes the target, is protected by a heatshield. The heatshield can withstand the searing temperatures while coming down and hitting the enemy target. Scientists like to describe this missile with pride. It is an awesome nuclear-capable intermediate range ballistic missile and is a terrific weapon of its time. The first stage of this missile is boosted by a motor derived from the SLV-3. More than 500 scientists who were involved with the *Agni* launch were spending anxious moments at the launch complex.

Among the dignitaries who had arrived at Balasore to watch the flight was the then Defence Minister K.C. Pant. Taking a stroll with Kalam the previous evening, the minister asked him : "What would you like me to do to celebrate the success of *Agni* tomorrow ?" Kalam replied : "We need 100,000 saplings at the missile research centre, Imarat." Imarat was a relatively new centre at Hyderabad and a barren patch of land, unlike the beautiful verdant surroundings of the Satish Dhawan Space Centre, which is also a bird sanctuary. Kalam wanted India's missile research and launch complexes to be filled with greenery, trees and flowers. The great rocket genius had not lost touch with Mother Nature.

Agni on the launch pad at Chandipur.
Dr Kalam inspecting the project.

Meanwhile, in the mission control room at Balasore, the scientists were tense. They were glued to the computers analysing data which was flowing in from the launch pad. The countdown clock was ticking away and *Agni's* take-off time was coming nearer and nearer. Everything indicated that it would be a smooth flight.

The mission control room echoed to the launch countdown 10-9-8-7-6-5-4-3-2-1-0. At 7.10 a.m. sharp, *Agni* took off majestically and streaked away into the blue morning sky over Balasore district. The flight lasted for 600 seconds exactly. Everyone felt a sense of tremendous adventure at the success of the *Agni* mission. The excited scientists clapped heartily and even carried their inspiring leader, Kalam, on their shoulders in a mood of joy. In this atmosphere, the memory of the two failed launches was temporarily forgotten.

As *Agni* rose higher and higher, its designer regarded it as one of the greatest moments of his life. Personally too, the success of his efforts gave him a tremendous sense of satisfaction. Soon, everyone around him could guess that it was *Agni*, which was very close to his heart. He had personally christened the missile *Agni*, which means 'fire' and had begun

Dr Kalam and his jubilant team after the successful launch of *Agni*

to refer to it as his dream project. Inspired by its success, Kalam broke into verse and penned these lines:

Do not look at Agni
As an entity directed upward
To deter the ominous
Or exhibit your might.
It is fire
In the heart of an Indian.
Do not even give it the form of a missile.
As it clings to the burning pride of this nation
And thus is bright.

This super success, drew world attention on India's scientific and defence capability. The US tried to compel India to refrain from carrying out similar launches in future as it felt that our country would become too powerful. But the government stood firm and continued with the programme keeping in view its national security interests.

The launch of *Agni* ushered in an era of heightened confidence among the scientists. The nation celebrated its 44th Independence Day with the successful test firing of *Akash*, followed a few days later, by the maiden flight of *Nag*, a third generation anti-tank missile. They redefined India's spirit of self-reliance.

President R. Venkataraman, who earlier as Defence Minister had approved the missile programme, cabled his congratulations. He paid rich tribute to Kalam's dedication, hard work and talent. Prime Minister Rajiv Gandhi called the *Agni* launch "a major achievement ...".

On Republic Day 1990, Kalam and Dr. Arunachalam were conferred the Padma Vibhushan by a grateful nation.

As the missiles thundered skywards, Kalam and the scientists felt a heady exultation. With each successful flight, they felt their confidence lifting higher. Thanks to Kalam, space research in India had matured to a heroic phase.

> "You should have an aim, a bigger aim and you should sweat and work with perseverance to achieve it."

11 POKHRAN II

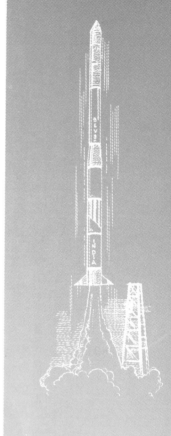

The success of *Agni,* the deadly nuclear capable missile, meant more to India than just a scientific gain. The media started calling Kalam 'India's Missile Man' and he became every school child's science hero.

To call Kalam a man of science alone is an understatement. He has been in the forefront of India's overall development for more than half a ntury. In recognition of his valuable contribution to the nation, he was awarded the Bharat Ratna, in 1997.

Being an action-oriented person, he did not sit back. There were still more things to be done. The *Agni* missile was ready. Now, the nuclear device which *Agni* could carry, had to be designed. India needed to have the capability to design a nuclear weapon which the missile could carry. Earlier on May 18, 1974, India had detonated a nuclear device at Pokhran. It reflected India's interest in using nuclear power for civilian constructive uses in peace time. It was done as per the terms of the Third Geneva Conference on peaceful uses of Atomic Energy (1964). But in 1998 apart from using nuclear power for peaceful purposes, India opted to induct nuclear capability in its defence.

When Mr Atal Behari Vajpayee became the Prime Minister in March 1998, he was firm on

Dr Kalam receiving the Bharat Ratna
from President K.R. Narayanan

BHARAT RATNA

The Bharat Ratna ('Jewel of India' Award), is given to a select few in recognition of public service of the highest order and exceptional contribution in the fields of Art, Literature and Science.

The announcement of the Bharat Ratna award to Dr Kalam in 1997 created a stir. A host of journalists and cameramen immediately flocked to Kalam's office in the Ministry of Defence, as he was then the Scientific Advisor to the Defence Minister. Taken by surprise by this sudden and unexpected development, Kalam became a little confused in his reaction. "When I heard I had won the Padma Bhushan ..." he floundered. The media understood the embarrassment of this shy scientist. Soon he had recovered his composure.

Instead of speaking about his achievements and his great contribution to the nation, Kalam, the missile guru, began to speak about Indian Science in the 21st century. He outlined future projects needed for India's defence – "high quality reusable supersonic missiles having stealth technology," he said. "We also need rockets which will use air as fuel. This would make the rockets lighter and also increase their range," he added.

Besides speaking of a future vision for India, this rocket hero did not in his moment of glory, forget to pay a glowing tribute to his team of scientists. "My achievement is part of my work as a team," he emphasised.

He also remembered the individuals who had forged his life and its success. The award for him brought back memories of his parents and his beloved teachers as well as scientists like Dr Sarabhai.

India following the example of the nuclear club comprising US, UK, Russia, France and China, at least with regard to nuclear weapon capabilities. He reasoned that possessing nuclear weapons would be to India's advantage because her enemies would think twice before launching an attack. Therefore, these weapons would essentially play the role of deterrents. Secondly, it would place India on a par with powerful countries. According to Mr Vajpayee by having nuclear weapons, India would not be viewed as a timid and weak nation by big countries.

The challenging task of making India a powerful nuclear-weapon state was entrusted with two most important people. They were R. Chidambaram, who was at that time Chairperson of the Atomic Energy Commission (AEC) and Abdul Kalam, who had then become Scientific Adviser to the Defence Minister.

As the nuclear programme began to pick up momentum, Prime Minister Vajpayee convened a meeting with Chidambaram and Kalam on April 12, 1998. After having discussions, he asked them how many days of preparation would be needed to carry out the nuclear tests. Spontaneously, Kalam, using the language of a rocket scientist, said: "T-30 days, sir." This means that the tests code-named 'Operation Shakti,' could be carried out at the Pokhran range in Rajasthan exactly 30 days after the scientists were given the go-ahead signal.

Vajpayee gave them the green signal. Immediately, they launched what is perhaps the most secret scientific operation ever conducted. It was jointly carried out by the Department of Atomic Energy (DAE) and the Defence Research and Development Organisation (DRDO).

For the success of the programme, a number of national laboratories were involved. Secrecy was absolutely necessary because if any of the super powers got a hint of this top secret project, they would have prevailed upon India to abandon the tests. Silence was the theme word. To ensure maximum secrecy, the scientists drew up the path of every civilian and military US satellite to identify the "blind spots", that is the days when these satellites would not be passing over Pokhran.

Scientists, electrical and electronic engineers, physicists, diagnostic and detonator experts and defence personnel, started moving to Pokhran with great care so the satellites could not pick up any movement. Some even travelled to Pokhran under assumed names, to avoid suspicion.

The nuclear devices which were to be tested were designed and developed at the Bhabha Atomic Research Centre (BARC) in Mumbai. Only a handful of scientists were involved in the actual nuclear weapon programme and they too were sworn to complete secrecy. They had to spend long hours at the laboratory. Once they were ready, the precious cargo had to be taken from the BARC laboratory to Pokhran.

BARC

The Bhabha Atomic Research Centre (BARC) which is located at Trombay in Mumbai, was the brain child of Dr Homi Bhabha, the father of India's nuclear programme. Dr Bhabha took a personal interest in designing the centre because he felt that with an indigenous nuclear programme India would become a powerful nation. This centre, which was started on January 3, 1954, was originally called the Atomic Energy Establishment. It was renamed Bhabha Atomic Research Centre on January 12, 1966 after Dr Bhabha's death.

Over the years, BARC has done work in different scientific disciplines, including medicine and agriculture. BARC has played a major role in increasing the share of the nuclear power programme for generating electricity and lighting up the rural areas of the country. BARC is, however, chiefly known for successfully conducting the Pokhran tests both in May 1974 and May 1998.

On May 1,1998, just after 2 a.m., when the roads of Mumbai were comparatively empty, the nuclear devices were taken in army vehicles to the Santa Cruz airport. The army vehicles reached the airport and stopped near a waiting Indian Air Force AN-32 aircraft which was parked at one end of the runway. From here the devices were to be flown to the safety of the IAF base at Jaisalmer in Rajasthan. The place where the weapons would be tested was a few hours further from there, by road.

The Pokhran range is a huge dry arid area in the heart of the Thar desert, 106 km from Jaisalmer. It is an extremely inhospitable terrain during summer when the searing heat proves merciless. A part of it is used for testing nuclear devices, another area has been earmarked for the Indian Air Force and the remaining, for the Army to carry out its exercises.

Flying over the zone in a helicopter one can just see an endless stretch of sand and no activity can be seen below. It is the last spot where anyone would like to be in the month of May.

According to those scientists who have been associated with the nuclear-weapon programme, poisonous snakes and scorpions were not an uncommon sight in the place. At night the scientists had to be extremely careful while making final preparations for the tests because there was every chance that they might accidently step on a snake or scorpion. Inside the tents, finishing touches were being given to the devices, under the light of lamps. There were also occasional sandstorms which made working in Pokhran very difficult.

The location of the structures where they worked were covered with sand dunes and dry grass in order to camouflage them. As the desert of Rajasthan has an undulating landscape, these artificial mounds appeared natural formations. Therefore, from outside there was nothing special about the place to suggest that there was some activity in progress in the zone.

There were pits dug by the Army in this zone. The nuclear devices which were to be tested were placed deep underground in these pits so that the radioactive fallout during the tests would be contained within the pits. For the sake of secrecy the pits were given code names like the *Taj Mahal*, *White House* and *Canteen*. The scientists even had to learn coded phraseology while discussing the forthcoming tests.

In the days prior to the tests Kalam and the scientists spent most of their time supervising the preparations in the scorching heat. To maintain complete secrecy, Kalam and other top scientists including Chidambaram wore army uniforms. Kalam was called Colonel Prithviraj. He was given that name after the highly successful Surface-to-Surface *Prithvi* missile, which is an effective weapon of peace and security. Also, Prithviraj Chauhan was a great Rajput ruler and every Indian holds him in great esteem. He was a romantic figure in Indian history.

The D-Day was fixed for Monday, May 11, 1998. It was Buddha Purnima Day and the scientists were hopeful of the results of the tests. But that morning there were strong winds blowing over the desert and the tests had to be postponed. The scientists, sitting on plastic stools in the control room, waited impatiently for the winds to drop to a mild breeze. They wondered whether the weather would oblige.

Kalam prayed that it should happen and his prayers were answered. At about 3 p.m., he telephoned the Prime Minister's office in New Delhi and informed the officials that the winds were dropping to a mild breeze and the devices could be tested in the next sixty minutes.

As Kalam gave the signal for testing, two officials, one representing the Department of Atomic Energy and the other the Defence Research and Development Organisation, turned the keys on a monitor. This instantly flashed a signal to the pits where the devices had been placed.

The bombs exploded at 3.45 p.m. They went off successfully and the scientists were thrilled. It was the world's 2048th test. It measured 4.7 on the Richter scale and the energy released was 53 kilo tonnes of TNT. The blast took place 150 to 200 m below the surface and the scientists monitored them from 5 km away. Kalam and Chidambaram, the two key figures of the nuclear weapons tests shook each other's hands. Within a few minutes the world awoke to a new and powerful India. They came to know that India had become a nuclear weapons country.

Prime Minister Atal Behari Vajpayee, Defence Minister George Fernandes, Dr Kalam and the scientists in victory mood after the success at Pokhran

As was his habit during intense moments, the success of the tests inspired Kalam to deliver an instant poem. He said: "I rejoiced when we shook the earth and broke it under our feet. I also felt that we had broken the nuclear power domination. Now nobody could tell our nation of a billion people what to do. It is for us to decide."

The spirit of infectious elation among the scientists at Pokhran was quite understandable.

Kalam and the other scientists managed to keep the tests away from the prying eyes of the powerful spy satellite operated by the American secret service agency, the Central Intelligence Agency (CIA).

CIA

The American Central Intelligence Agency (CIA) was created in 1947 with the signing of the National Security Act by President Truman. It obtains secret information about foreign countries, mainly about their defence programmes, political developments and matters relating to security. For this purpose it employs human spies as well as satellites.

Its headquarters is located in Virginia near Washington DC. The CIA keeps a keen watch on countries developing nuclear weapons.

To accomplish its mission, the CIA engages in research, development and other hi-tech scientific systems.

This formidable satellite had the capability to even detect the movement of an ant on the ground. But, on May 11, 1998, it failed to spot the successful Indian nuclear weapons tests.

The spy satellite had mistaken the preparations for the nuclear tests to be the setting up of another military outpost in the border area of Jaisalmer. The scientists lived in tents and travelled in military vehicles. This camouflage had been effective.

Kalam conveyed the news of the successful nuclear testing to an anxious Vajpayee. When it became public, it shook the world. US intelligence called their failure to detect the secret preparations the 'intelligence failure of the decade'. In India, the announcement of its success electrified the nation and the Prime Minister congratulated the scientists and engineers who had been responsible for its success.

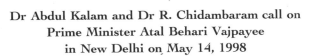

**Dr Abdul Kalam and Dr R. Chidambaram call on
Prime Minister Atal Behari Vajpayee
in New Delhi on May 14, 1998**

Two days later, on May 13, smaller nuclear devices were tested. Throughout the programme the cover of secrecy had been strictly followed.

The period of triumph for Kalam continued. Congratulatory messages began to pour in from various corners of the country. People representing different walks of life praised him for making India a powerful nation with rockets, missiles and nuclear bombs.

Some also questioned the need for such tests since India was the birthplace of Mahatma Gandhi, an apostle of non-violence. Kalam explained the significance of the tests while speaking to journalists in New Delhi. He told them that after the success of the tests India had become a strong country which no one would dare to attack with a nuclear weapon. He called the launch of the nuclear-weapon programme a national mission and a challenging one. He emphasised that nuclear weapons were solely for the country's national security.

The success of the tests had earned Kalam various titles. Often he would be called 'Mr Nuke,' or the 'Father of the Nuclear Bomb'. But, he wanted to ensure that these titles did not mean that he was making the country an aggressive one. He was keen on making it clear that these weapons were solely for peaceful purposes. The opportunity came during an interaction with children at the Rashtrapati Bhavan on November 14, 2002.

He explained to the children that India would never be the first to use nuclear weapons against its enemy. They would be used only if some other nation attacked India with nuclear weapons and threatened its peace. He told journalists that war had been averted between India and Pakistan because both the countries had nuclear weapons.

For the success of the missile and nuclear tests, the government elevated him to the rank of Principal Scientific Adviser. He now began to focus on different scientific issues. From this point his life and career took a new turn.

12 KALAM AND KIDS

The success of the strategic missile launches and nuclear devices made people, especially those in the government, realise that Dr Kalam had a golden touch. There was a growing feeling everywhere that India's advances in the aerospace sector were mainly due to the efforts of Dr Kalam. The community of scientists and the intelligentsia in the country knew the work of this visionary and they expressed the view that Kalam's services should be utilised further. The government also felt the need to make use of his talent and expertise to harness technology for transforming Indian society.

The government offered him the post of Principal Scientific Adviser in November 1999. Even earlier, during the Pokhran tests period, he was serving simultaneously as the Chairman of TIFAC (Technology Information Forecasting and Assessment Council), an autonomous body under the Department of Technology. The major task of TIFAC was to look ahead to the advances in technologies worldwide and to keep India abreast of the changing times. In its tasks TIFAC networked with the government, industries, scientific and technological organisations, as well as financial institutions and intellectuals. For eight years Kalam led a team of 500 experts in TIFAC and evolved

Technology Vision 2020. Later, the *Technology Vision 2020* and the national security aspects got combined into *Indian Millennium Mission 2020* (IMM 2020). It aimed at transforming India from a developing to a developed nation by 2020. As the Principal Scientific Adviser, Dr. Kalam focussed on evolving a plan for implementing *IMM 2020.*

The marathon meetings he held with his colleagues helped to achieve a consensus on the importance of each branch of science in improving the various sectors of society and thereby contributing to the welfare of the nation. But, initially, the focus would be on five sectors : These were agriculture, power, education and healthcare, information technology and the strategic sector. Dr. Kalam felt that emphasis on these five areas would help in transforming India into a developed nation by 2020.

As Principal Scientific Adviser, Kalam travelled all over the country meeting people from all walks of life and inspiring them to be partners in realizing *Vision 2020.* He felt that an important stratum of society needed to be addressed—the youth of India. He felt the need to personally interact with them.

A child greets President Dr A.P.J. Abdul Kalam in Bhuj

He therefore left his job as Principal Scientific Adviser and moved to Chennai to fulfil his wish and took up research and teaching at the prestigious Anna University, his alma mater. This provided him with a lot of intellectual satisfaction because he could speak to the younger generation and share with them his thoughts.

During this period, he began to travel all over the country addressing school students. He always said that he felt rewarded and comfortable in their company. He had set himself a target of meeting 100,000 children. By November 14, 2002, he completed this target.

Prior to starting a session with children, he makes them recite a song which he has specially composed for them. He has called it the *Song of Youth* and titled it, **Me and My Nation – India.**

> As a young citizen of India,
>
> armed with technology, knowledge and love for my nation,
>
> I realise, small aim is a crime.
>
> I will work and sweat for a great vision,
>
> the vision of transforming India into a developed nation
>
> powered by economic strength with value system.
>
> I am one of the citizens of a billion,
>
> only the vision will ignite the billion souls.
>
> It has entered into me,
>
> the ignited soul compared to any resource,
>
> is the most powerful resource
>
> on the earth, above the earth and under the earth.
>
> I will keep the lamp of knowledge burning
>
> To achieve the vision ... Developed India.

Once they have finished reciting it, Dr Kalam asks the children to pose questions to him. He finds the questions interesting and thought-provoking. The questions reflect the children's inquisitive minds. Everywhere, they look forward to the arrival of their own 'Uncle Kalam' because he never talks to them like a stern schoolmaster. Instead, he plays the role of a pupil while students become teachers putting questions to him. The mood is always relaxed and informal and the children enjoy themselves thoroughly.

On his part Dr Kalam feels delighted that he can satisfy the curiosity of the youngsters. He even allows the children to ask him questions on subjects which are not at all related to science or technology. They are curious to know about his hair style, his interests and hobbies and eating habits. He answers all of them enthusiastically with the familiarity of a dear uncle. With this avuncular approach children never for a moment feel that they are meeting him for the first time.

During a visit to the Anandalaya High School at Anand in Gujarat in April 2002, a question came up from the audience, "Who is our enemy ?" Liking this question Kalam encouraged the children to come forward with their views. There were many answers. But, the reply of a 12th Standard girl, Snehal Thakkar impressed him the most. She said India's main enemy was poverty. To express his appreciation, he dedicated his book *Ignited Minds* to her. He also invited her personally for

Snehal Thakkar at the Rashtrapati Bhavan with President Dr Kalam

the swearing-in ceremony at the Rashtrapati Bhavan when he took over as the President of India on July 25, 2002.

Another question from a student of the same school set Dr Kalam thinking. The questioner wanted to know whether the weapons which Pakistan had made were more powerful than those made in India. Dr Kalam reflected over the question for a while. He wanted to give this child a truthful and correct picture of India's position. He assured the youngster that India had the capability to design, develop and produce any type of missile and nuclear weapon, but would not be drawn into an arms race, pitted against Pakistan.

Regarding the role of the *Agni* missile, he told a student at Bokaro that it was not meant to destroy any country since no country is India's enemy. He explained to him that the purpose of developing *Agni*, was to display India's strong technological capabilities. Dr Kalam said that a strong India meant that our country and the surrounding areas would remain a zone of peace and the nuclear armoury would serve as a deterrent.

At a Tripura school he was asked about the importance of role models. He told his students that the best role models are their parents and teachers. He also asked them to emulate the example of astronaut Kalpana Chawla. According to Dr. Kalam, Kalpana Chawla would always remain a source of pride for everyone. He also had a word of advice for the parents and teachers. He urged them to guide children to be good human beings. He urged teachers to open the windows of knowledge and not to stifle creativity.

Elsewhere, at Dindigul in South India, he emphasised the importance of dreams. He said dreams will transform into thoughts which in turn will convert into actions. He told the children that success would always follow dreams though there could be a few setbacks.

At Pune, on May 28, 2003, Dr. Kalam jointly read a poem with Rimanika — a seven-year old girl from J.B. Petit High School, Mumbai.

Rimanika of J.B. Petit High School for Girls reading her poem along with Dr A.P.J. Abdul Kalam at Symbiosis Institute at Pune, in May 2003

The poem was written by Rimanika herself.

> "Tomorrow is a better than a thousand yesterdays
> With a vision in your heart and mind
> You are sure to find a rainbow of your dream in your mind.
> With a vision you are sure to filfill your dream
> A vision in your mind makes you very intelligent
> A vision in your mind will always stay a vision
> The eye of vision will always be a single vision
> And will not change into double."

While replying to questions at a school in Tezpur in the north-eastern part of India, he said that the vision of a *Developed India by 2020* called upon the youth of this country to launch a mission to connect rivers, cutting across states. This project would benefit states like Rajasthan and Tamil Nadu which did not have enough water.

During a session at Cuttack, he was asked about his favourite books. He answered that they were *Man The Unknown* by Dr Alexis Carrel, Thiruvallur's *Thirukkural, Light from Many Lamps* by Lillian Eichler Watson and the *Holy Quran.*

Interaction with children has been the greatest enjoyment for Dr Kalam.

13 THE ROAD TO RASHTRAPATI BHAVAN

It was the evening of June 9, 2002. Dr. Kalam was at the Anna University having discussions with his students, who were working for their doctorates, when the telephone rang.

To his utter surprise, the caller was Prime Minister Atal Behari Vajpayee. Dr Kalam wondered why the PM was telephoning him. Was it something to do with his project to make India a developed country by the year 2020? Or, did he want to talk to him about some important scientific project? After the exchange of pleasantries, Dr Kalam waited expectantly for the PM to bring up the matter. What Dr Kalam heard from the Prime Minister was something quite beyond his guesses. Would Dr Kalam consider to be the ruling party's Presidential candidate? Vajpayee asked.

Rashtrapati Bhavan

Did he hear him right? For a moment Dr Kalam wondered if he was dreaming. He was too stunned to give an immediate response. Then he recovered himself, thanked the PM and said he would be only too happy to accept the offer.

Mr Vajpayee and the ruling alliance chose Dr Kalam as the Presidential candidate because of his outstanding achievements, his apolitical background, simple lifestyle, love for children, and his strong commitment to the nation.

Of course Dr Kalam was not elected unopposed. Pure political reasons made the Left Front put up Dr Lakshmi Sehgal as their candidate though they had great esteem for Dr Kalam as a person.

Unlike earlier Presidential candidates, Dr Kalam sent a letter to all the MPs and MLAs outlining his vision for a Developed India. It read: "It speaks for the power and vitality of India's democracy that a poor boy from a small island in Tamil Nadu can travel this far in the service of the motherland and now be considered for the responsibilities of Rashtrapati Bhavan."

He emphasised his vision and mission which would be to :

* Eradicate poverty, promote agriculture, agro-based and cottage industries.
* Encourage greater participation of women in Parliament, state legislatures, political and public bodies.
* Accord top priority to national security.
* Strengthen friendship with all countries in the world.
* Consider and keep Jammu and Kashmir an inseparable part of India.
* Focus more on the principle of secularism.
* Endeavour to work for bringing about unity of minds among the people of India.
* Preserve the country's natural resources.
* Give a boost to literature, music, arts, crafts and sports.
* Help the youth of the country.
* Make India a knowledge super power so it can face the challenges of increasing competition in various sectors.

He concluded his note saying that he was optimistic that India would become a developed nation by the year 2020 because of "India's youth and India's children."

A few days before the election he addressed a press conference which was also quite unprecedented. His first words to the journalists were: "Smile, smile does not cost you anything. It is a beautiful day." The sober countenances of the journalists, which would have otherwise gone well with the occasion, melted into a hundred smiles by the sheer radiance of this sparkling piece of welcome.

He then said: "From last Sunday [the day on which the PM telephoned him in Chennai], till today the whole process appeared to me like the launch campaign for a rocket system to put a satellite into orbit or a missile system to reach its target."

Dr. Kalam made it clear that he would retain his simplicity amidst the pomp and glory of life at Rashtrapati Bhavan.

Asked about his scientific activities after assuming the office of the President, he remarked: "When I am elected as President, I will try to see how technology can be used to develop the nation. Election as President does not mean *sanyas* from science."

Pointing out that he has always worked as a scientist in different areas like putting satellites in orbit and developing nuclear technologies, he emphasised his main focus would be on attaining self-reliance in the fields of science, commerce and industry.

Dr Kalam also remarked: "I can only say that we should try whether religion can graduate into spiritualism.... managers can graduate into leaders and political leaders turn into political leaders with compassion, and the education system work towards cent per cent literacy."

He ended the press conference by saying that he would consult the country's leading constitutional experts on controversial issues.

A few days after this interaction came the day of the election — July 15, 2002. Dr Kalam seemed relaxed and told the mediapersons: "I feel fantastic and I am looking forward to my victory."

When the counting of votes began, those opening the ballot papers found some interesting messages on them wishing Dr Kalam the very best in his Presidential career. Some said that Dr Kalam should trim his hair so that he would look like a real President !

Three days later came the announcement. Dr. Kalam was declared elected, exactly 22 years after he had successfully launched the SLV-3 rocket from the Satish Dhawan Space Centre in Sriharikota with the *Rohini* satellite in orbit. Of the 4,785 MPs and MLAs who voted, Dr Kalam secured 4152 votes. July 18 has always proved a lucky date for him.

PRESIDENTIAL ELECTION

The President of India is indirectly elected. The election is carried out according to a system of proportional representation and by means of a single transferable vote from among an electoral college. The electoral college consists of the elected members of both Houses of Parliament and the members of Legislative Assemblies of the states. To secure uniformity of quantum representation among states as well as to keep parity between the centre and the states, suitable weightage is given to each vote. The candidate receiving an absolute majority of the voters' first preference vote, is declared elected.

As the news spread, there were celebrations throughout the country. In Rameswaram, where Dr Kalam was born, there was a festive mood. His photograph was displayed everywhere. Outside the famous Sri Ramanathaswamy temple, autorickshaw drivers decorated the streets with festoons. *Archanas* and *aartis* were performed at the temple.

At the mosque, where Dr Kalam used to offer *namaz* as a child, people offered special prayers for the success of his Presidential career. At his home in Mosque Street, there was a flood of visitors congratulating Dr Kalam's 87-year-old brother, Mohammed Muthu Meeralabha.

> *"As President, I will be able to contribute towards the development of the country by interacting with people representing various disciplines and working with various segments of the population. In my opinion the post of the President reflects the integrated aspirations of a nation."*

14 THE SWEARING-IN

As the day for the swearing-in — July 25, 2002 neared, Dr Kalam began preparing for it. From his tailors at Karol Bagh, he ordered four closed-collar Jodhpur suits (*bandhgala*) in his favourite colours, black, navy blue, steel grey and beige.

His unconventional hairstyle had been a topic of conversation. His hair stylist Javed Habib opined that it suited a rocket scientist, but snipped a few inches to suit a President.

The countdown for the function had started. Among those Dr Kalam had personally invited to attend the swearing-in ceremony in the Central Hall of Parliament House, were 34 people from Rameswaram, including his elder brother, Meeralabha.

Travelling to New Delhi, in the train, Meeralabha kept counting the beads of his rosary. For P.V.L. Sastri, a 24-year-old temple priest, it was one of the greatest moments in his life because he was carrying special offerings from the Rameswaram temple for Dr Kalam.

At the New Delhi railway station, the Kalam family attracted the attention of a large number of curious onlookers and the media. Dr. Kalam remained untouched by the excitement of the masses and the media attention. The day of the ceremony started like

**Relatives and friends of the President-elect A.P.J. Abdul Kalam
aboard a train to New Delhi to attend the swearing-in ceremony**

any other day with the regular 5 km walk at the Asiad Village, his home in New Delhi. He had a shower, ate a light South Indian breakfast consisting of idli, sambhar and buttermilk. Then dressed immaculately in a *bandhgala* suit he stepped out to acknowledge the greetings of the crowd gathered outside. And, there were hordes of cameramen and TV crew members who focussed on him as he drove to Rashtrapati Bhavan. Accompanied by the outgoing President K.R. Narayanan, Dr Kalam was welcomed at Parliament House by the then Vice-President Krishna Kant and Lok Sabha Speaker Manohar Joshi.

Among the galaxy of invitees were Prime Minister Atal Behari Vajpayee, Deputy Prime Minister L.K. Advani, former Prime Ministers I.K. Gujral and H.D. Devegowda, the entire cabinet, Chiefs of Army, Navy and Air Force, Opposition leaders, industrialists, former President R. Venkataraman, Dr. K. Kasturirangan, Dr. R. Chidambaram, colleagues from the science fraternity, and 100 school children including teenager Snehal Thakkar who was the inspiration of his book, *Ignited Minds*. In order to accommodate the large number of invitees, the swearing-in ceremony was held at the Central Hall for the first time.

**Dr A.P.J. Abdul Kalam being sworn in as President of India
by the Chief Justice of India, Mr Justice B.N. Kirpal, on July 25, 2002**

The Home Secretary Kamal Pandey read out the communication from the Election Commission about the election of the new President. Dr Kalam took the oath in the name of God.

Watched by television viewers across the country, 70-year-old Avul Pakir Jainulabdeen Abdul Kalam was sworn-in by the Chief Justice of India B.N. Kirpal as the 11th President of India. A 21-gun salute boomed in the background. He was now the country's First Citizen and Supreme Commander of the Armed Forces.

In keeping with Dr Kalam's motto of doing things speedily, the ceremony started before the scheduled time of 10 a.m. and lasted just an hour and 18 minutes. For the swearing-in ceremony of previous Presidents it had taken a longer time.

In his brief speech after taking the oath, the new President quoted the first lines from a *kriti* of the legendary music composer Thyagaraja: *"Endoro mahanuhavulu andariki vandanamulu"* (I salute all the great human beings with all my heart) and stressed the need for "a collective vision" to tackle the challenges faced by the country. This is the time to ignite the minds of the people for this movement to make India a developed nation.

He then quoted a line from Kabir's poem which said: "What you want to do tomorrow, do it today, and what you want to do today, do it now."

The ceremony ended with the National Anthem.

Once all the ceremonies were over, Dr Kalam drove to Rashtrapati Bhavan in the Presidential cavalcade escorted by the President's Bodyguard. He was given a guard of honour by a contingent of the Army, Navy and Air Force.

With a warm smile and obliging the watching mediapersons constantly clicking shots and calling, "Once more, President Sir," India's rocket hero took over office as the 11th President of the Republic of India. As the First Citizen of this land, Dr Kalam declared : "Now we need a movement in the country. This is the time to ignite the minds of the people for this movement. We will work for it. We cannot emerge as a developed nation if we do not learn to transact with speed."

The People's President

RASHTRAPATI BHAVAN

- The famous architects Sir Edwin Lutyens and Sir Herbert Baker were given the task to design the Rashtrapati Bhavan. Work for its construction started in 1913 and was completed in eight years.

- The Rashtrapati Bhavan covers an area of 18,580 square metres. The total cost involved in the construction was Rs. 1.4 million. Over 3,500 men worked on 99050 cubic metres of marble, and 1,700 million bricks went into its construction.

- The overall design concept of the building is a fusion of traditional and European architecture. The dome is a virtual replica of the Sanchi Stupa.

- Its first occupant, was the Viceroy Lord Irwin, who moved in on January 23, 1931. It has been the home of five Viceroys of the British Raj and 11 Indian Presidents.

- It was known as the Viceroy House when India was governed by the British. After the country gained independence on August 15, 1947, it was renamed as the Government House. On January 26, 1952, it was called the Rashtrapati Bhavan.

- The magnificent palace apart from being the residence of the Indian President has played host to several visiting heads of states and governments.

- It has one of the largest gardens in the country, the Mughal Gardens, which consists of 1384 sq. metres.

> *"My story is a story of a scientist tested by failures and setbacks; the story of a leader supported by a large team of dedicated professionals."*

15 RECOLLECTIONS

(The author recounts the start of his association with Dr Kalam in the article published in the Bombay Times *on July 25, 2003.)*

Kalam ko Salaam

Srinivas Laxman

On May 22, 1989, India successfully test-fired a powerful nuclear-capable intermediate range ballistic missile called *Agni*. This flight is of personal significance to me because it marked the start of my friendship with the man behind this awesome missile, A.P.J. Abdul Kalam, now our very popular President.

Our friendship began with a telephone call I made to him at Hyderabad and congratulated him on the success of the flight. Going by my experience with other scientists in Mumbai, I expected a brusque reply from him. Instead, I found him to be a soft-spoken person. He thanked me profusely and in a tone full of humility, said his team deserved full credit for the success.

Over the years, we kept regularly in touch. Sometime ago my wife Usha and I undertook what may be called a 'Kalam Pilgrimage' to Rameswaram – the birthplace of our President. We visited his house on Mosque Street where he was born. It was a small house which indeed reflected his humble beginnings.

An old man standing in the verandah viewed us with a mixture of curiosity and suspicion. When we explained that we had specially come to Rameswaram because we were admirers of Kalam, he invited us into the house. We talked for a while and took photographs with him. We sent a copy of the pictures to Kalam, then the scientific adviser to the defence minister in New Delhi. When we spoke to Dr Kalam later, he said he was deeply moved by the fact that we had taken the trouble to visit his hometown.

In January 1999, during our visit to Delhi with our daughter Rimanika, I telephoned Dr Kalam and said I wanted his autograph on his super autobiography, *Wings of Fire*. He agreed and said he would meet me at the hotel where I was put up.

When I met him and inquired if he could come up to my room for a while, he readily agreed. As we were nearing the lift, a hotel security guard stopped us and wanted to know details about the person accompanying me. Without getting annoyed, Kalam gave his name and said he worked with the defence ministry. The guard then asked Kalam to enter his name in a register and then allowed us to proceed.

Kalam decided to leave and we came down to the lobby, and there was literally a guard of honour for him given by the hotel staff. The security guard who had questioned him sincerely apologised admitting that he was not aware that he was after all *the* Kalam. The scientist asked him not to bother. He in fact praised him for doing his job properly. "We need more people like you," he told him.

I find absolutely no change in him after he became the President. There cannot be a better example of this than what happened on February 15, 2003, at the Shanmukhananda Hall when he interacted with nearly 3,000 school kids. The programme was organised by the South Indian Education Society. Setting aside protocol, he moved freely with the children talking to them. When he saw me, he gave a warm handshake and a hug, saying. "Where have you been, my old friend ?"

Recently in Pune, when my daughter presented her poem to him, he read it along with her, appreciated it, and within a week, even sent her a warm reply. This is the President we have.

K. KASTURIRANGAN
Former Chairman of Indian Space Research Organisation

"I met Dr Abdul Kalam for the first time in 1965 when I was doing research at the Physical Research Laboratory in Ahmedabad. At that time Dr Kalam was in charge of developing the uppermost stage of India's first satellite launch vehicle, the SLV-3.

"I recall that when a few of our engineers received acid burns during a test in the 70s at Thumba, some officials were checking the administrative procedures to admit the injured to authorised hospitals. Dr Kalam shot back telling that the engineers be immediately admitted to whichever hospital they would think fit and if the procedures did not allow reimbursing the expenses, he would bear the cost out of his own pocket. What is more, he saw to it that each of the injured was looked after by two of his own colleagues in the hospital."

"At one point he became the head of the Defence Research and Development Organisation and I headed ISRO. I had to visit New Delhi periodically for meetings.

"After a day of continuous meetings, we used to settle down in a restaurant which offered good food which Dr Kalam enjoyed. His favourite eating places were the Coconut Grove restaurant at Hotel Yatri Nivas and a South Indian restaurant at Lodhi Hotel.

"Since Dr Kalam was a regular visitor to these restaurants, the waiters used to know him and always made it a point to reserve a table for him. The children who were in the restaurant recognized Dr Kalam and used to flock to our table and request him for his autograph. Dr Kalam used to willingly give it to them and also tell them in a light-hearted manner that they take my signature too in their autograph books."

"I invited him for my son's wedding at Tiruchchirappalli." He came to the marriage, blessed the couple and ate with everyone. Later Dr Kalam even came to our house. When he became the President, my daughter-in-law exclaimed : "Is the new President, the same uncle whom I had served masala dosa ?"

"When I was working on designing a remote sensing satellite and we had to develop the Polar Satellite Launch Vehicle (PSLV) which will carry it, Dr Kalam and I used to have a lot of discussions on how the rocket should be designed. He used to call me every 15 minutes to discuss the best possible design for the PSLV. Thanks to these intense interactions we developed a rocket which is versatile and successfully proved its capability.

"During these discussions, he displayed a restless mind resulting in him always putting counter-questions. He is a very good listener, very receptive and very attentive to what you are saying. I must say that talking to him is a very stimulating experience."

G. MADHAVAN NAIR
Present Chairman of ISRO

"Dr Kalam was the project director of the SLV-3 programme. He used to hold the review meetings which used to begin at 4 p.m. and go on till 10 p.m. After a hard day's work we had to stay awake and during those days there was no proper canteen at Thumba. To ensure that we were alert, Dr Kalam used to bring a kettle with black coffee and distribute it to us ! He stayed in a single room which was full of books. He was a voracious reader.

"The technical committees consisted of scientists who had their own egos. Dr Kalam in his own gentle and subtle manner used to put an end to these egos successfully synergised various groups.

"On August 10, 1979, when the first SLV-3 flight failed, he took the entire responsibility. When it succeeded on July 20, 1980, he gave the credit to the entire team. That is Dr Kalam."

S. SURYANARAYAN
Aerospace Engineering Department, Mumbai IIT

"In 1996, Dr Kalam was invited to deliver the convocation address at our institute. He had already arrived and he telephoned me to say that he will be in the institute by 3.30 p.m. since he had some work in the city (Mumbai). I did not know what to say and I mentioned this to Dr S.P. Sukhatme who was then director of our institute.

"Dr Sukhatme was concerned because he wanted Dr Kalam to join him for lunch along with the board of governors. He mentioned this to me. I wondered what to do. I telephoned Dr Kalam that the students of the aerospace engineering department would be extremely disappointed if he did not meet them.

"This did have a magical effect on Dr Kalam. When he heard the word 'students,' he instantly changed his mind. He arrived at our department at 12 p.m. and interacted with the students. It was a lively and interesting session. Thereafter, in the afternoon he gave the convocation address to a large audience in the auditorium to which everyone listened in rapt attention.

"Ten years earlier, when Dr Kalam was the Director of Defence Research and Defence Laboratory in Hyderabad, I went to attend a meeting there. On landing at Hyderabad airport from Mumbai, I was waiting for some of my colleagues who were due to arrive by a Bangalore flight. While I was waiting, Dr Kalam spotted me, inquired about my well-being and asked me if I had transport to proceed to the venue of the meeting.

"When I told him that arrangements had already been made, he still went out of the terminal, identified the driver along with the car which was to take me to the meeting venue and informed me. He did this despite the fact he was boarding a flight for Bangalore."

KOTA HARINARAYANA
Former Director of Light Combat Aircraft (LCA) Project
Vice-Chancellor, Hyderabad University

"I would like to describe Dr Kalam as a 24-hour man who virtually worked round-the-clock. He had no value for clocks.

"I remember when the LCA was taking shape, Dr Kalam used to convene a meeting in New Delhi at a guest house. We were based at Bangalore and after finishing work for the day we used to catch the late evening flight to New Delhi, arrive there, have dinner and prepare ourselves for the meeting which used to begin at 11 p.m. Generally it ended at 2 a.m.

"We then used to catch the early morning flight back to Bangalore, and return to our offices by 9 a.m. We were very enthusiastic and so never felt tired.

"And I recall those days when Dr Kalam attended meetings at Bangalore to review the LCA project. He used to land at Bangalore from New Delhi at 11 p.m. and proceed directly to the shop floor to check the progress of the aircraft programme.

"It was a complex project and critical issues had to be resolved. I give credit to Dr Kalam because he maintained his cool and never for once got angry or lost his temper on such occasions.

"During the meetings, he used to say that he was never afraid of problems. He used to say that a person is a master of his own problems and he used to drill this point to us continuously.

"When the US imposed sanctions in 1998, we had to evolve a new strategy to complete our projects. This is where Dr Kalam's project management skill came to the fore. He was an excellent manager."

G.S. RAUTELA
Director, Nehru Science Centre, Mumbai

"We had invited Dr Kalam to speak to school students to commemorate National Science Day at our centre on February 28, 2002. The hall was jam packed and the students eagerly heard him. Afterwards they put a lot of questions to him, which he answered. While interacting with them he got delayed for his return Indian Airlines flight to Chennai. I was accompanying him to the airport to see him off. At Mahim, we were caught in a thick traffic jam. I was almost certain that Dr Kalam would miss his flight. I was getting tense. I requested him to allow me to use his mobile phone to call the IA airport manager to delay the Chennai flight. Dr Kalam almost caught my hand to tell me that I should not do that."

"I remember another incident at Ahmedabad in 2001. After the board of governors' meeting of the Vikram A. Sarabhai Community Science Centre in Ahmedabad which Dr Kalam chaired and I attended as a member, we were travelling together to Ahmedabad airport in the same vehicle. Dr Kalam asked me, 'Sir, what is your core competence ?' I was really surprised at the humility of Dr Kalam addressing me 'Sir'."

KAVITA GADGIL
Mother of Abhijit Gadgil, a MiG-21 pilot who was killed in a crash

"On August 5, 2003, at 1 p.m. I was ushered into the highest office of this country. The man sitting behind a large desk got up and walking around it, strode briskly towards me and greeted me with a smile, but effective welcome, "Kavitaji, please come." He was unwell, but still kept his appointment.

"After welcoming me and my family members whom he later called an Air Force family of which we felt justly proud. I then told him about the alarming state of MiG-21 aircraft safety record in the Indian Air Force and about our son Abhijit who was killed in a MiG-21 crash.

"Then I gave him my petition which ran into some four pages. He read all of them and amazingly he did not seem to need glasses to read. While he read, we looked around his very high ceilinged office; very spartan, very functional but warm.

"His desk had a few files and many books and by the side stood a computer which was on. There was a copy of the *Bhagwad Gita.* My gaze also fell upon the painting depicting Gandhiji with the Indian tri-colour being unfurled at one side. We could also see mementos of military hardware.

"He then reassured us that flight safety in the IAF will show a positive ascent."

VASANT GOWARIKAR
Former Director of Vikram Sarabhai Space Centre from 1979 – 1986

"On February 21, 1969, we launched a rocket with a new type of propellent and the rocket's hardware was given by Dr Kalam. The mission was a success. There was only one thing in his mind and that was work. He expected all of us be the same way, though he was a very congenial person."

V. SHANKAR
Secretary, South Indian Education Society, Mumbai

"Dr Kalam had invited me for the swearing-in ceremony and I reached New Delhi the previous day. He was staying in the Asiad village. When I went to meet him I found a huge crowd and a large number of securitymen. It was extremely difficult to go through them.

"I then sent a slip to him through his staff. He saw my name, and immediately came down and met me. We then adjourned to a room on the ground floor and talked for one-and-a-half hours despite his busy schedule. Everyone else was wondering how I managed to get him down !"

R. ARAVAMUDAN
Former Space Director, Satish Dhawan Space Centre, Sriharikota

"I first met Dr A.P.J. Abdul Kalam in 1963 at NASA's Wallops Island launching facility in Virginia. I was already there with three other colleagues. Dr Kalam joined us a few months later. A few months later after training we returned to India.

"As the years rolled by, most of us got married. Only Dr Kalam resisted all our efforts to get him hooked. Even after his family gave up, his friends persisted. All of us were constantly talking about hiring a couple of buses to take us from Thiruvananthapuram to Rameswaram for his wedding. But, it never happened. He gave us all the slip and remained wedded to his work.

"After I got married, he would often come to our house. He loved traditional Iyengar food. As soon as my journalist-wife and I landed in Thiruvananthapuram, he (Dr Kalam) lent her his old Royal portable typewriter which stayed with us for several months. He would love to talk about his favourite book, *Atlas Shrugged*, and its hero who was his ideal.

"In those days, he would also talk about his dream of building a hovercraft in his backyard. He always intended to take a house with a big yard and get to work on it. Somehow that too never happened. The SLV-3 project got going and it took all his time.

"Later when I became Director of Sriharikota Launching Station, he would often come there to test some of his sub-systems. He would invariably stop by our house for lunch and talk about old times.

"During those days, he was not particularly religious. He was at ease with all his friends of varied religions. He has always loved Tamil since his initial schooling was in Tamil. He was a voracious reader of Tamil magazines and books. Later on, he even began writing Tamil poetry.

"Dr Kalam always took himself very seriously and was earnest about whatever he did. He would throw himself completely into a project and motivate others to work as hard as he did.

"When we rang up to congratulate him on his nomination as President, my wife asked how he would have reacted if someone had stopped him on the streets of Thiruvananthapuram in the 1960s and told him he would one day become the President of India. 'I would have laughed,' he replied, 'It was something so unimaginable,' he said."

THE ACADEMIC RECOGNITION OF ABDUL KALAM'S CONTRIBUTION TO THE NATION

Dr Kalam has been conferred doctorates by the following universities.

Doctor of Science

- Anna University ● Jadavpur University
- Kalyani University ● University of Hyderabad
- Benaras Hindu University ● Roorkee University
- Mysore University ● IITs – Mumbai, Delhi and Kanpur
- Birla Institute of Technology, Ranchi ● Allahabad University
- Indian School of Mines ● The Maharaja Sayajirao University of Baroda
- Bharathidasan University, Tiruchchirappalli ● Universities of Chennai and Delhi
- Manipal Academy of Higher Education ● Andhra University, Vishakhapatnam
- Madurai Kamraj University ● Chhatrapati Shahuji Maharaj University, Kanpur
- Tezpur University ● Rajiv Gandhi Proudyogiki Vishwavidyalaya, Bhopal
- Visveswaraiah Technological University, Belgaum

Doctor of Philosophy

- Jawaharlal Nehru Technological University, Hyderabad

Doctor of Literature

- Dr. Babasaheb Ambedkar Marathwada University, Aurangabad

Desikottama – D. Litt Honoris Causa

- Viswa Bharati, Santiniketan, West Bengal

SOME IMPORTANT AWARDS WON BY DR ABDUL KALAM

1981 – Padma Bhushan for 'Distinguished service to the nation'

1990 – Padma Vibhushan for 'Exceptional and Distinguished' service to the nation

1996 – Prof. Y. Nayudamma Award for his role in encouraging science in the country's industrial development

1996 – G.M. Modi Award for 'Innovative Scientific Research'

1996 – H.K. Firodia Award for 'Excellence in the field of Science and Technology'

1997 – Bharat Ratna – The country's highest civilian honour

1997 – Indira Gandhi Award for promoting National Integration

1998 – Veer Savarkar Award for 'Science and Technology'

2000 – Ramanujan Award for 'Science and Technology'

OTHER AWARDS

- Dr Biren Roy Space Award for playing an important role in the field of Space Technology

- Om Prakash Bhasin Award for Science and Technology

- National Nehru Award of the Madhya Pradesh Government for Science and Technology